HOW TO SET UP AND RUN A SUCCESSFUL AIRBNB BUSINESS

OUTEARN YOUR COMPETITION WITH SKYROCKETING
RENTAL INCOME AND LEAVE YOUR 9 TO 5 JOB EVEN IF
YOU ARE AN ABSOLUTE BEGINNER

FRANK EBERSTADT

CONTENTS

INTRODUCTION

The longer you're not taking action the more money you're losing.

— CARRIE WILKERSON

Imagine a life in which you get to visit the most beautiful and interesting places in the world. Imagine meeting new people, visiting historic sites, hiking beautiful trails, and finding local treasures. People want to have these kinds of experiences. Back in my single days, I lived that life and saw parts of the world that others could only dream of visiting. Then, after marrying my amazing wife and starting a family, I got to share my travels with my wife and kids. You might be wondering how this was possible. The truth is, if it weren't for Airbnb, I wouldn't have had these experiences and been able to see the world in so many unique ways.

As a solo backpacker, you don't have much money for travel—the main goal is to see the world's amazing sights. You also want to meet people and experience culture by immersing yourself in it—you want to stay where all the action is. Then, when you trade this life in for growing a family, you have to be more conscious of the little ones. Vacations become more about spending time with your family and enjoying the immediate surroundings. While you might still have a few adventures here and there, the main goal is to connect with your family in a special place. Being an avid traveler in both stages of my life allowed me to stay in a variety of Airbnbs—I know what works and what doesn't.

If all the traveling adventures weren't enough, we decided to make a huge move that came with many challenges and so many beautiful memories. We picked up our lives and emigrated to the Land Down Under.

Shortly after arriving in Australia, I knew I wanted to be in the accommodation business—I started working for an investment group that operated hotels and motels. Alongside this, I established my own property business. You could say that I have a passion for property and travel. What better way to combine these two than with Airbnb?

If you are someone with the same interests, then Airbnb is definitely for you. It provides a unique opportunity to deliver a fantastic travel experience to other people. If you have traveled before, you will know what a huge difference accommodation can make. I know that, out of all my travels, the accommodations were the travel experiences that I enjoyed the most.

If there was anything I wanted to make money from, it would be through properties. I loved the industry, and I knew that so many other people did as well. Everybody wants a fantastic vacation. There are so many complexities when starting a business and building an additional income that you want to enjoy the process—this is why Airbnb is such a great opportunity. Hosting people is an absolute pleasure if you know how to do it right. Not only that but investing in property means you have future security. Not only will you make an income, but you will always have your property to fall back on if you ever need additional income or a place to stay—a terrific method for maximizing control over your finances and avoiding economic unpredictability.

Currently, I have six properties and still work for the investment group I mentioned earlier. I'm quite experienced in the real estate industry, and more importantly, I have an Airbnb business. Throughout my time in this industry, I've learned quite a few lessons, and I've had to do them independently. That is the more challenging option, but you don't have to take that route. The knowledge that has taken me twelve years to accumulate, I want to pass on to you so that you can build up your Airbnb business and have it run smoothly without going through all my ups and downs.

When you start an Airbnb business, you will be able to become financially stable and simultaneously enjoy the process. When you become an Airbnb host, you open your doors to the rest of the world. The types of people you meet, the experiences you will have, and the stories you will get to tell all add to the wealth-building you will be participating in. Developing an Airbnb business is an investment in a better future for you and your family. By now, you are probably itching to find out how you can step into this journey so let's dive straight into Chapter 1.

1

AIRBNB BASICS

O ver 150 million users worldwide have booked over 1 billion stays using Airbnb[1]. That is a lot of people who are looking for a unique and convenient place to stay when they go away. The traveling market has opened up, and people are looking for more affordable places to stay when they are traveling. It is essential to understand the basics of Airbnb before you can move on and create a strategy that will help you tap into all the benefits that come with it.

WHAT IS AIRBNB?

In the simplest of terms, Airbnb is an alternative to hotels. It allows individual property owners to list and rent their properties or rooms via the platform. The average property owner has access to a whole list of new clients they would not have otherwise. It also allows guests to find new, interesting, and often, inexpensive options for their vacation, business, or other travel needs. Before, you would need to be a hotel or a large rental chain to get enough business. Now, any person who has an available property can rent it out and make additional income.

The origin story of Airbnb is quite interesting. To say that it was something intentional wouldn't be true. It all started in 2007 when Brian Chesky and Joe Gebbia were completely broke and looking to make some extra money.[2] They lived in an apartment in San Francisco and needed a way to help pay their rent. They discovered a conference happening in their area and decided to rent out an empty room with an air mattress in their apartment for some extra cash. They called the service "AirBed & Breakfast." As you can see, this is where the name originated. Over a few years, this small idea grew, with the help of Nathan Blecharczyk, into the Airbnb platform we know today.

It is easy to look at the company and think it was an easy ride. Everybody loves to travel, and doing it uniquely and cheaply makes sense, right? However, the conception of this idea was purely accidental. When they were trying to build up the company, people genuinely thought they were crazy. Very few people thought this would be a good idea that would be profitable in the future. If you look at it in the context of 2007 or 2008, who wants to pay money to stay on an air mattress? They struggled to get investors to buy into their idea.

While you can see things from the investors' point of view, the people booking with them were telling a different story. People were even sharing their resumes and LinkedIn profiles to show that they were responsible and not security risks. They wanted a unique spot to stay, and this was when the founders believed they were onto something. After a while, they were accepted into a start-up accelerator program in San Francisco called Y Combinator, one of the points where the company pivoted. The idea suddenly started to catch fire and gain traction.

Airbnb has opened up real estate investing to the general public. You can make some money even if you are a recent graduate with only a small property. You don't even have to own the property yourself. Many renters are able to utilize

Airbnb to make some extra money. It has opened up a whole new world for travel and for making extra money for yourself.

HOW IT WORKS

Airbnb is an interesting concept. One important thing that people often misunderstand is that the Airbnb platform does not own any of the properties that are advertised on the website. Most of the control is left up to the host. The host will decide if they are comfortable with the offer, the price, and many other aspects of their rental property. The Airbnb platform is simply the intermediary between the guest and the host. Some rules and regulations need to be followed to ensure that the guests have the best experience possible and the hosts are protected.

Guests

If you have stayed in an Airbnb before, you will probably understand how it works for a guest. It's a pretty straightforward process, and it's user-friendly. To utilize the platform as a guest, you just set up an account on the platform.

Once your profile is complete, you can scroll through the listings until you find a property you like and want to stay in. Since there are millions of listings on the platform, you can utilize the filters to help narrow it down, so you're not scrolling for hours. Guests can view pictures, amenities, features, and descriptions of the various listings to better understand what they are getting into. There are also reviews left by previous guests. This helps each guest get a better idea of what the service is like and what other people's experiences have been. The higher the rating, the better the experience is likely to be.

Once the guest finds a listing that they like, they can go ahead and book it. There are additional prompts that they are taken through to pay and confirm the booking. In most cases, the booking request goes to the host to be confirmed, and then the payment process will continue. The exception to this is if the listing has an instant booking option. This allows them to skip the host verification step and book immediately.

Hosts

The process for a host is a bit more detailed because you have to create your listing and ensure everything is in order. There are plenty of options for Airbnb hosts, so regardless of the type of property you have, you will likely find an option that will suit you. You can rent out an entire property, just a room, a shared room, or a specific portion of the property. There is even an option to list events on the platform.

You will need to create an account with Airbnb. This account is completely free, but in some areas it may vary, so it is a good idea to look at the fees and restrictions that will affect you. Certain areas might also have restrictions on Airbnb or rental properties in general. It is wise to research if any of these apply to you and your property. To complete your account, you will follow the prompts and upload the necessary documents and files. You will also need to ensure that your listing looks attractive so people will want to book with you. This means you need to write a description, upload pictures, and create a title for your listing. You will also be able to set a price. The price is completely up to you, but it is a good idea to set a competitive price, as setting it too high won't get you that many bookings.

You will also be directed to a calendar function where you can indicate when your property will be available to rent out. Some people only rent out their property during certain months; others do it throughout the year. It is completely up to you, so you can decide what will work best for your schedule. Once you have completed your information and followed all the prompts, you can publish your listing. Then, all you have to do is wait for people to start booking with you. This is just the basic overview of how Airbnb works for a host, but we will dive into more in-depth steps throughout the book.

IS AIRBNB SAFE?

One of the biggest concerns that people have is whether Airbnbs are safe or not. The platform creators have developed many systems and tools to ensure the safety of both guests and hosts. Identity verification, reviewing procedures, and private internal messaging make it much safer for both parties. Since payment is made through the platform, money can be held until check-in. This provides security to the guest, as they know they will not lose their money. Many people are scared of being scammed, so the fact that the host is not paid until after check-in reassures the guests.

Multiple verification methods are put in place for both hosts and guests. Both will have to enter personal details that must be confirmed. As a host, you can see how much information somebody has uploaded. The more information somebody provides, the more trustworthy they are likely to be. The same goes for guests who are looking for trustworthy hosts. The review system is an incredibly valuable part of the platform. Both guests and hosts review each other. This means you will be able to see any negative reviews about a potential guest, and they would be able to see the same about you. This helps you to make better choices when you are accepting a booking request.

With all of this being said, there have been some Airbnb horror stories. Before this puts you off, consider the fact that Airbnb is a massive company. There are likely to be a few bad experiences with the millions of properties worldwide that advertise with Airbnb. Airbnb does its best to help mitigate the situation and ensure that any guest or host that does not meet the standards is permanently removed. Since Airbnb cannot be in direct contact with every guest and every host, it is best to ensure that you take precautions to ensure your safety. We will be diving more into the nitty-gritty of this in later chapters.

DIFFERENT TYPES OF AIRBNB ACCOMMODATIONS

One of the biggest draws of Airbnb is the fact that there are many different types of accommodations for a guest to choose from and that a host can list. This gives incredible flexibility to all parties. Understanding the types of accommodation you can list on the platform will allow you to make better investment decisions, especially if you are looking to purchase a new property to list on Airbnb.

FOUR MAIN TYPES OF PLACES OFFERED VIA AIRBNB

Airbnb offers extreme flexibility for a host. You can rent out any type of space as long as customers are looking for that particular type of rental. There are four main types of places that Airbnb offers. We're going to dive into these now.

- **Entire Place**: The traveler will book the whole property for themselves and will not have to share the space with anybody else. An entire property could include a garden, a pool, and other amenities.
- **Private Rooms**: This is a larger property divided into common areas for the guests. A guest will have their own bedroom and possibly bathroom, but share the other amenities with other guests.
- **Hotel Rooms**: These are simply hotel rooms that are rented out on Airbnb.
- **Shared Rooms**: This is similar to hostel-style living. It is targeted more toward younger travelers because it will be a room with multiple beds where the amenities are shared by everyone.

SPECIALIZED ACCOMMODATIONS

In addition to the four main types offered on Airbnb, there are many specialized accommodation types that you can list. This provides even more flexibility to both the host and the guests.

Airbnb for Work

This is a spinoff from Airbnb, which allows corporations to use the platform to make bookings for business trips. It allows a business to plan trips for their employees and to keep track of the bookings that have been made. The more 5-star reviews that your property gets from business travelers, the more likely it will show up on Airbnb's work trip feed. There are also a few other criteria that need to be met in order to show up on this filter. For example, you would need to have high-speed Wi-Fi, well-equipped workstations, after-hour access, be close to transportation and cities, and possibly offer on-site laundry facilities. All of this provides for the needs of a business person who is traveling into town for a meeting or other business purpose.

Airbnb Plus

Airbnb Plus is reserved for the finest quality homes with great reviews. In order to become an Airbnb Plus host, you will need to be verified by Airbnb. There will also be an in-person inspection to make sure that you fit the criteria. You will definitely need to put in some extra effort in order to gain this status. It comes with additional maintenance requirements as you will need to provide above and beyond what other Airbnb hosts generally offer. This might mean that you need to ensure that your kitchen is stocked with amenities like cooking oil, basic cooking supplies, dishes, and cutlery. You might also need to stock your bathrooms with hair care products, bubble bath, high-quality bathing products, and other amenities. Your property also needs to have something different about it. Exceptional design is part of the qualifications that are required.

Airbnb Luxe

This option allows travelers to access amazing properties as well as trip designers to help them plan their experience. These homes are hand-picked from around the world and pass a very strict verification process. Standards need to be met in both design and function, as well as 300 different criteria. This is not just about offering guests great accommodation, but ensuring their trip is transformational and unforgettable. It is essentially about creating an experience.

Unique Stays

Many travelers out there are looking for unique experiences and uncommon spaces to rent out. These are non-traditional properties or spaces that can be rented out on the platform. There are so many types of unique stays that are available, so if you have a property that fits the bill, you will be able to utilize it for Airbnb. Perhaps you have a houseboat, a yurt, or a tree-house. There are even igloos are available on the platform.

Properties Run by Superhosts

In order to achieve Superhost status, you need to complete 100 nights of hosting over three completed stays or have ten completed stays over a period of a year, maintain a 90 percent response rate, have less than a 1 percent cancellation rate, and maintain a rating of 4.8. There are many guests out there who adjust the filters to look for Superhosts. Since a Superhost needs to meet these additional criteria, the guests can be sure that they are in for a good experience. It is definitely worth your while to try and earn this status.

It does take a bit of work to get there, but if you can maintain quality standards you will be able to become a Superhost. There are many incentives that are offered when you are a Superhost. You will be able to charge a bit more in your pricing since you have been verified and meet the higher standards. You will also get dedicated Airbnb support, improvement in listing visibility, and a badge signifying your Superhost status.

The fact that there are so many options available on Airbnb means that you will likely find one that's going to work for you. You can offer specialized accommodation or simply fit into one of the four primary categories. Either way, you will be able to make some good money through Airbnb if you utilize the right strategies. In the next chapter, we are going to be looking at being an Airbnb host and what it is really like.

THE TRUTH ABOUT AIRBNB HOSTING—MYTH VS. REALITY

Many people are put off from using Airbnb because of the many myths that surround it. It is really helpful to be able to see what is true and what is a lie. This way, you will be able to move into your Airbnb journey with confidence.

MYTH 1: THE VACATION RENTAL INDUSTRY IS SKETCHY

There are so many people out there who think the vacation rental industry is sketchy. The truth is that vacation rentals have been organized by individual property owners for many, many years. The only difference between Airbnb and other privately owned vacation rentals is that the platform makes it a lot easier for people to connect with each other. Airbnb is simply a place for property owners and travelers to meet. Previously, it was a lot more difficult to find a private property owner who offered a unique place to stay. Now, it is just more convenient.

MYTH 2: BEING A HOST MEANS YOU CAN'T GO ANYWHERE ELSE

A common myth is that you will never be able to leave your property. If you are somebody who loves to travel and spend time away from your home, this belief may keep you from pursuing an Airbnb business opportunity. However, there are plenty of options available to you if you want to leave your property and travel. In most cases, you are not going to be expected to stay on-site while you have guests. Unless you are providing a service to them each day, you really don't need to be there to babysit. This is especially true if you have private property or private rooms that are being rented out. Most of the time, people want to be left alone, so if you have ensured that everything is up to date and maintained on your property, then you are not likely to need to be there at all.

With this being said, it is always a good idea to have somebody available who will be able to assist your guests if necessary. You could hire a property manager to handle all the affairs of your property while you travel and do the things you enjoy. Another option would be to have a friend or someone else that you know take care of the property while you go on holiday.

MYTH 3: AIRBNB IS ONLY PROFITABLE IN THE WEST

If you do not live in the west, a common myth is that your Airbnb is not going to be successful. This is definitely not true. Although Airbnb was started in San Francisco and founded by Americans, it has expanded to the rest of the world. There are over 7 million active listings across the world. These listings span 100,000 cities in 220 countries and territories.[1] There are millions of hosts worldwide, and they are making good money out of it. People want to be able to travel all over the world, not just in the west. Airbnb has a global approach to ensure that it thrives all over the world. You will be able to receive payment in your local currency and the platform allows you to process those payments easily.

MYTH 4: AIRBNB GUESTS ARE MOSTLY PARTY PEOPLE WHO CAUSE TROUBLE AND DESTROY FURNITURE

This myth is fueled by a few horror stories that have come to light. The truth is, there have been some bad experiences for hosts who have had to deal with crazy partygoers who have ruined their property. With 103.7 million stays in the second quarter of 2022 alone, if there are one or two bad experiences that come out of it, it really is not that much.[2] Not only that, but Airbnb does take these things very seriously and will ban guests from using the platform if there is a reason to do so.

Even if you do have a bad experience with a guest at your Airbnb, the chances that it will be a massive blow to your income and your property are quite small. When dealing with people, there's always going to be the possibility of having a bad guest experience. These things are quite easy to handle and typically blow over. If you take the time to screen your guests before you confirm the bookings, you shouldn't really have an issue finding decent houseguests. Communication is always important so that you can set the standard for what you expect from your guests. This will prevent potential miscommunications down the line.

MYTH 5: BECOMING AN AIRBNB HOST IS ONLY ABOUT BUSINESS

Some people truly want to run Airbnb as a business, and that is completely valid. However, there are other people who do not want to do that. Either way, how you want to run your Airbnb is going to be completely up to you. Becoming an Airbnb host is not solely about business. When it first started, it was about offering experiences and making connections. If this is your main motivation, then this is what you can offer to your guests. Of course, making a profit is a big part of running an Airbnb, but your true motivation could lie in the hospitality side of it.

Airbnb is different from traditional hotels and formal vacation rentals. You are allowed to make it feel as homey as you would like. It is an expression of your creativity and hospitality. People know that when they book with Airbnb, they are not going to get a crisp, clean, and formal experience. They'd rather get something that feels a bit more personal. If you are passionate about hospitality and want to open your doors to strangers so that you can form new connections and relationships, then let this be your motivation and run with it. That extra-special personal touch is what has gotten many people 5-star reviews.

MYTH 6: AIRBNB RENTALS ARE BAD FOR MY NEIGHBORHOOD

People love comfort and things that stay exactly the same. The problem with this is that comfort does not often lead to growth or improvement. If you look at anything good that has happened over the past few years, you will see that it came about due to some sort of change. Many people are quite afraid of inviting Airbnb rentals into their area because they think it's going to lead to neighborhood deterioration. This is definitely a myth, and the opposite is actually true. When you invite more tourists into your area, you are spurring on the economy. You're leading to more economic growth for small businesses and for the people who live in the neighborhood.

Adding new people to the area also introduces diversity and allows for new thoughts and ideas. You will find that neighborhoods that open themselves up to new cultures and experiences are ones that tend to grow. If a neighborhood has growth potential, then more money would be invested in it, and the quality of life would increase for those who live there.

Of course, this can be a scary process if you are somebody who is not used to change, but it is absolutely worth it because the positives definitely outweigh any potential negatives. Airbnb is simply an advancement of an already established industry. It is something that has always existed but has now been improved upon. In the next chapter, we will look at helping you decide whether starting your own Airbnb business is the right decision for you.

9 SIGNS STARTING AN AIRBNB BUSINESS IS RIGHT FOR YOU

To date, Airbnb hosts have earned more than $150 billion. With 14,000 new hosts joining every single month, that number is only going to increase.[1] While this is enticing, it is important to understand whether Airbnb is right for you. Here are a few things you should consider and ask yourself before moving forward.

SIGN #1: YOU HAVE A KNACK FOR HOSPITALITY

Hospitality is definitely a talent, and there are many people who have it. If you are somebody who genuinely enjoys hosting people and doesn't mind playing hotel manager, then this could be the perfect fit for you. You will be able to invite many different people from all over the world into your home. You can cater to them and ensure that they are having a good time while they staying with you.

SIGN #2: THE MARKET CONDITIONS ARE THERE

Above all, Airbnb is designed to help you make some money. If you're unable to make a profit, it is definitely not going to be worth your time and effort. This is why it is so important to understand the market conditions where you are. There should be enough demand in your area or in the area you are looking to purchase a new property. This demand should be sufficient to facilitate your business and make financial sense.

You should have a look at whether your property is somewhere that people want to stay. This is why it is so important to do research about your area. It doesn't make sense to start an Airbnb and put all your time and effort into it if nobody wants to book in your neighborhood. Areas that have a high demand for tourism or business travelers tend to do better with Airbnb because there is a constant stream of people booking with you. Have a look to see how many other Airbnbs are in your area or how many other rental properties there are in general. Then see if they have a high occupancy rate. This just means how often the properties are booked out. That will give you a good idea about the viability of an Airbnb business in your current area.

SIGN #3: YOU'RE IN IT FOR MORE THAN JUST A QUICK BUCK

Building an Airbnb business takes some time. You are not going to be raking it in from the first moment you click publish on your listing. As with any business, it does take some patience in order to develop a successful long-term business. If you are not somebody who is able to put the necessary time and effort into your Airbnb business, this might not be the right option for you.

SIGN #4: YOU HAVE ENOUGH STARTING CAPITAL

An Airbnb business is not something that you can start up with absolutely nothing in your bank account. You need to have some start-up capital in order to get your property ready or purchase a new one. If you are looking to purchase a new property to start your Airbnb business, then you will need a good amount of start-up capital. Even if you are going to be hosting a property that you already own, you still need money to get your property Airbnb-ready.

Airbnb is not just about simply renting out an extra room in your house. You need to be able to create an experience for your guests. This means that you need to purchase new linen, furniture, and decor. You are trying to create a good experience for your guests, so you can't just use anything that you find in your house. You will need to purchase plenty of new things in order to get those good reviews from your guests. If you simply throw in the old lounge set from your 20s and the bed that you no longer use because it is now uncomfortable, you are not going to be able to run a successful business. Start-up costs are just part of the deal when it comes to running any successful business.

SIGN #5: IT'S ACTUALLY ALLOWED IN YOUR JURISDICTION

Not every area is going to be welcoming to Airbnb. There are various legalities, rules, and restrictions that might come into play depending on your area. You need to ensure that your Airbnb business will be legal. Make sure to check locally to ensure that you are allowed to run an Airbnb out of your property. You should also ensure that you understand the restrictions that apply if you are allowed to rent out your property as an Airbnb. This is definitely one of the biggest things that you should consider when getting into Airbnb. You might need to purchase a property outside of your current location in order to start up your business.

SIGN #6: YOU HAVE ENOUGH TIME AND ENERGY

It is definitely possible to start up your Airbnb as a side hustle, but you do need to have time to put into it. This is especially so when you are trying to get things off the ground. You'll need to make sure that your property is good to go, and this does take some time and effort. Once your property has been listed on Airbnb and is ready to receive guests, you need to have time to tend to your guests' demands and turn over the property for new guests. Maintenance and cleaning are all part of the deal when it comes to running an Airbnb, so you need to take this into consideration.

SIGN #7: YOU'RE OK WITH THE COSTS

It is so important that you are realistic about the costs involved with running an Airbnb. There are definitely one-time costs that need to be considered. However, the costs don't just stop once you have listed your home on Airbnb. There are recurring costs that need to be taken into consideration when you are running your business. For example, you would need to provide your guests with certain things in order to help them enjoy their stay. Perhaps you are providing them with a welcome basket, shampoo, body wash, basic cooking essentials, basic cleaning essentials, and similar items. All of these things will need to be replaced once they have been used.

You might also need to think about bringing in a cleaning or maintenance service to help you out. This is also going to incur costs. This is why it is important for you to sit down and make a budget for yourself so that you understand exactly how much money it is going to cost you to run an Airbnb business. This will help you prepare for the future and make sure that you have a realistic idea of how much profit you will be making.

SIGN #8: YOU HAVE ENOUGH RISK TOLERANCE

Like with any business, there are some risks to take into account when you are investing in an Airbnb business. There are financial and personal risks that come with this kind of endeavor. You need to be completely honest with yourself and sit down to discover what level of risk you are comfortable with and if this is the right option for you.

SIGN #9: YOU ARE COMFORTABLE WITH STRANGERS IN YOUR HOME

There are some people who are quite touchy about letting strangers into their personal and private spaces. This doesn't mean that you are not a hospitable person. It just means that you are uncomfortable with people invading your space. If this is the case, then Airbnb is probably not going to be the best option for you. Think about whether you are open to the idea of people you don't know using your facilities and sleeping under the same roof as you. It is completely understandable if this is not something that appeals to you. However, it is important that you be honest with yourself so that you don't start something that you, later on, find out that you just don't enjoy.

———

The truth is, being an Airbnb host is not for everyone. However, if you are willing to take the risk and if you have what it takes, the payoff can be huge. Running an Airbnb does have a monetary benefit, but the benefits extend far beyond this. You will be able to expand your knowledge and broaden your horizons based on the people that you invite to your home. It is truly an enjoyable experience if this is something you know you are well fit for. In the next chapter, we are going to cover the Airbnb framework that you can use to jumpstart your own Airbnb business.

THE "AIRBNB FRAMEWORK" FOR STARTING YOUR OWN SUCCESSFUL AIRBNB BUSINESS

You don't have to be a genius or a visionary or even a college graduate to be successful. You just need a framework and a dream.

— MICHAEL DELL

THE "AIRBNB FRAMEWORK"

The rest of this book is going to be organized into six separate parts. These parts are going to go through the framework for creating a successful Airbnb business. There will be a lot to cover in each of these sections, and when you put everything together, you will be able to run a very successful Airbnb business. In this chapter, we are just going to give a summary of what this framework is like for creating a prosperous Airbnb business.

Analyze (Chapters 6–8)

The first stage of this process is going to be analysis. Whenever you start a business, you need to have all the facts before you get going. This helps you to understand the environment and what your goals are. You will also need to look at the competition so that you can assess the viability of your business plan. Proper analysis is fundamental to any effective plan.

Insurance (Chapters 9–10)

When it comes to renting out a property, insurance is so important. If you do not have insurance, then you're putting yourself at risk of losing money and other valuable items. This is why we have to spend some time talking about insurance in general and what insurance you need to have.

Ready Your Property (Chapters 11–15)

The third step is all about getting ready for your guests. At the end of the day, an Airbnb business is all about the property and making your guests happy. If you are able to do this, you will encourage good reviews and get continuous business. This is an incredibly important part of the process and something that needs to be concentrated on. Another thing to note is that preparing your property is going to be a constant thing. You will always need to ensure that it is at its best at all times. This will make sure that every guest who steps through your doors has a great experience.

Booking Management (Chapters 16–19)

Being able to manage your bookings is an integral part of running an Airbnb business. You need to ensure that the process is easy to follow and efficient. This will remove a lot of stress from you and your guests and make it a lot easier to manage who stays in your Airbnb and all the details surrounding that process.

Get Noticed (Chapters 20–25)

Getting noticed is really important if you want to bring in as many new guests as possible. If your listing is not eye-catching and doesn't draw the attention of people scrolling through the platform, you will not be able to make a lot of money through Airbnb investing. This is why it is so important to do what you can to get yourself noticed. There are many strategies and tips that you can put into place, and in this section, you will be able to learn everything you need to.

Build Relationships (Chapters 26–27)

It is really important to develop good relationships with your guests. This will result in them wanting to come back and stay with you. If you have many returning guests, you will know that they will be taking care of your property, and you can trust them with your space. It also allows you to have more security in terms of bookings. You know that a few good people will be booking your property every once in a while. This is incredibly important to building a good business.

There are definitely many different paths that you can take when you are starting your own Airbnb business. The Airbnb framework is a very simple six-step process that will help you to start any Airbnb business from the ground up. It doesn't matter how much experience you have in hospitality or even building a business. In the next chapter, we are going to go over the first step of the process—analyzing the market.

STAGE 1

ANALYZING THE MARKET

HOW TO ANALYZE THE PLAYING FIELD

I n the US alone, there are over 660,000 Airbnb listings.[1] There are a ton of people who are making their dreams come true through real estate investing. There are different ways to identify who your competitors are and their place in the market. Not all of those 660,000 listings are successful. The ones that will be successful are the ones that put themselves in the most profitable position. This starts with being able to analyze what you are working with. Then you are able to make the right decisions for the current market.

TOOLS YOU'LL NEED

There are many different tools that you can utilize in order to help you with your analysis. These are easy to use and quite easy to access as well. Some of them might require you to pay some sort of fee in order to use them, but most of them are free.

AirDNA

The first tool we are going to be talking about is AirDNA. This platform provides research and analytics software. It helps you to understand how the short-term rental industry is changing over time. You will be able to dig deeper into the rental market using this tool. You can get trend reports and forecasts to help you make your decisions and understand exactly what is going on in your market. As a host, you will have access to granular insights that are behind the industry and the business.

AllTheRooms

This is a great tool that provides business insights and analytics. This is specific to the vacation rental industry. It includes multiple key features such as market intelligence, property intelligence, and competitive intelligence. This will help you to get a more in-depth look at what is happening in your area so that you are able to make better decisions regarding your rental property.

Facebook Hosting Groups

There are multiple Facebook hosting groups on the platform. You can join them and gain insight into what is going on in your market. It helps to connect with other Airbnb hosts so you can see what they're doing and what their strategies are. In most cases, other hosts are quite happy to share their knowledge and insights with people that are new to the market. If you can find a great community of people who are willing to give you one-on-one advice, this is going to be incredibly valuable to you. You can ask specific questions and get advice on what you are currently struggling with. It also helps just to have other people around you who are going through the same process. You will feel supported and most likely be able to develop better strategies for your Airbnb.

I have created a Facebook group for hosts to share, learn, get advice, and find support from other people who are going through the same thing. Everyone is welcome to join, so you can extend the invite to other Airbnb hosts you might know. This is a private group, so you can feel free to share, knowing that only the people who are going through the host journey will be able to see and respond. Please feel free to join. I would love to have you!

Here are the details:

Name: Airbnb Host Community

URL: www.facebook.com/groups/airbnbhostcommunity

QR Code:

FACTORS TO CONSIDER

When you are doing your analysis, before you start investing in Airbnb, you need to look at a few key factors. These factors will allow you to get a holistic view of how profitable your Airbnb will be. You will also be able to develop strategies that are specific to you, and that will let you know what will work for your area and your property.

Destination

When it comes to investing in property, location is key. Even if you already have a property that you want to turn into an Airbnb, you still need to understand the ins and outs of the location and if it's going to work for short-term rentals. If you think about it, people would rather stay in an average Airbnb that is located centrally to what they want to do and see than stay in an amazing property that does not allow them to see the sights they want to see or be surrounded by the environment they want to be in. This is why it is so important to think about the location. You can pretty much change anything about your property except for the location, so don't skip this step.

People often book holidays based on location and not on the accommodation that they're going to stay in. Once they decide on the location, they will then start looking for rentals in that area. This is not to say that the other aspects of your Airbnb are not important. It is just simply to note that location is typically the first thing that people consider, which is the reason why it is so important.

When you are looking at your current location or the location you want to invest in, you need to understand a few things. The first thing you should think about is seasonality. This means knowing when the high and low seasons are. When are people flocking to this area and when are people staying away? This will help you to understand the times of the year which will be the most profitable and why people are coming to the area at this time. It also allows you to price your properties appropriately at various seasons so that you can ensure you are making a good profit. Things like major holidays and events also impact how many people are coming to an area. If you live in an area that has big festivals or events, you know the people who want to stay at rental properties during this time.

Beyond simply understanding the important dates that guests are going to be coming to your area, you also need to understand what the place has to offer. Restaurants, sightseeing spots, landmarks, parks, and activities are all really important to the location. Guests will often look for local attractions and suggestions for things that they could be doing while they're in your city or your area. The better the facilities that surround your Airbnb, the more popular it will be. If your guest simply wants to relax and enjoy the time, it is reassuring to know that there are plenty of restaurants, stores, and activities around the property. This will result in a much better retention rate.

Target Market

The next thing to consider is your target market. This typically goes hand-in-hand with the location, as there will be a specific type of person that wants to visit a specific type of place. Not only that, certain people will gravitate toward certain types of properties as well. If you understand who your target audience is, then you will be able to tailor your property to meet their needs. You should be realistic about who this target market is as there are going to be some limitations based on your property.

Certain types of people will be more attracted to certain cities, areas, and properties. Your city's tourism website as well as active Airbnb listings will give you a good idea of the demographics. Think about whether your city attracts more leisure tourists or business people. If tourists frequent the area, you can think about whether these tourists are coming in groups, families, singles, or couples. Think about what kind of amenities they are looking for and what they are willing to pay for these amenities. All of this information will help you tailor your property to what your target guests need. This will help you with marketing as well as the general provisions of your property. You will also be able to understand what kind of people are going to be staying with you.

Local Regulations

Many cities and states have decided to regulate rental properties and alternative lodging in different areas. This means that
every property investor needs to understand the regulations in
the area they want to invest in. You don't want to be put in a
situation where you get in trouble with your local government
for not sticking to the rules. You also don't want to put all this
money into your Airbnb, only to realize that you have to shut it
down a few years or months later. It is a good idea to consult
your municipality and HOA to get all the information that you
need about your property and what you are allowed to do.
Once you have this information, you might have peace of mind
in your area, or you might need to look into investing in
another city or state.

Competitors

Understanding your competitors in the area is really important.
You can do this by finding a few similar properties and using
them as a benchmark for yours. Make sure that the properties
you look at are ones that are offering the same type of service
that you are. It's not really going to make sense to compare
yourself to a five-bedroom, self-catering house when you have
a two-bedroom guest house. Look for properties that are going
to be your closest competitors and go from there.

You will need to look for competitors in the same or nearby
neighborhoods. The properties need to have a similar configu-
ration to yours. This just means having the same number of
bedrooms, bathrooms, and comparable amenities. Once you
have found a few properties that are similar to yours, you need

to do some investigation. Have a look at how many competitors there are in your area. If there are too many, you might struggle to get guests. If there are too few, it might be a good idea to find out why there aren't as many Airbnbs in that area. You can also have a look at the pricing and how much of the calendar is open. The pricing will give you a good idea of what people are charging. If you look at the calendar, you will be able to see how in demand the area and the type of property are. You can cross-examine the pricing and the calendars. This way, you can get a good idea of what pricing gets the most bookings.

It is also a good idea to have a look at the reviews that are on the properties. Try and find out why the reviews were good or bad. This way you will be able to avoid bad ratings and provide your guests with the things that they were missing in the other properties. Once you have evaluated your competition, you can have a look at your own strategy and see what you need to change. You might notice that your pricing is not optimal for the market, and you can tweak this a little. Perhaps you could look into providing a few more amenities for your guests to enjoy on your property. Simply having a look at your competitors and what they are offering is a really good way to help improve your Airbnb strategy.

Financial Considerations

When you're investing, it means that you have to put some money in order to get money out. Your investment needs to make sense for you, and you need to be sure that you will be getting a good return on your investment. It is definitely a good idea to take the financials into consideration before you start investing or start putting your plan into practice. You can calculate your potential rental income, but you also need to understand the expenses that come with running your own Airbnb. All the money you make from your daily rates is not going to be just for profit. You will need to use some of that money to keep your property running smoothly and for other business costs.

Your financial considerations are not just going to be limited to purchasing a new property or renovating the one you currently have. There are going to be some continuous costs that you will need to take into consideration. These are going to be your expenses. Any money you make through your rental needs to be able to cover your expenses and then have a bit left over for your project. Here are a few things that you should be considering in terms of expenses you might incur while running an Airbnb:

- Inspection fees
- Repairs
- Furniture
- Insurance
- Utilities
- Maintenance
- Property tax
- Rental income tax
- Cleaning fees
- Hosting fees

This is definitely not everything that you need to consider when it comes to your expenses. However, it gives you a good idea of what to expect.

When it comes to performing market analysis for your Airbnb, there are many things that you need to consider. The above factors will help you develop a plan and a strategy to better understand the market. You will find that making decisions is a lot easier when you have all the information in front of you. It might seem like a long and tedious task, but it is definitely worth it. In the next chapter, we are going to compare the different types of properties that you can rent out.

PROS AND CONS OF RENTING OUT DIFFERENT PROPERTY TYPES

Airbnb recently announced 56 new vacation rental categories for over 4.4 million of its listings.[1] This means that now, more than ever, it is important for first-time Airbnb hosts to think about their property and how they can make it stand out. Not only that, but it opens up the door of opportunity for you to rent out whatever kind of space you have. Some of the categories that have been opened up are camping, design, and amazing pools. If you have a property with a unique feature or that is in a unique area, you can definitely use this to your advantage and get noticed more.

Different types of properties will need different strategies to help them stand out. It is important to consider what type of property you have to purchase when you are getting into short-term real estate investing. In this chapter, we are going to take a look at the many different types of rental properties that are available. It will give you a good idea of the unique strengths and weaknesses of the various property types. This will allow you to make better decisions and create a better strategy for yourself going forward.

DIFFERENT TYPES OF RENTAL PROPERTIES

You might recall from Chapter 2 that there are four primary types of Airbnb accommodation. Along with this, there are more exotic types of accommodation available. With this being said, you will likely find similarities between unique stays and the four primary types of rentals that we are going to be talking about in this chapter.

Entire Place

The first option is to rent out the entire property. When doing this, your guest will have complete access to everything that is on the property. This might include the yard, pool, and all the other areas of the house. Renting out an entire property does not necessarily mean that it needs to be a house. You could also rent out an entire apartment, condo, or villa. However, there are some criteria that need to be met when renting out this type of property. Typically, a guest would be expecting a bedroom, cooking space, and a bathroom.

This is a great option for many guests because it allows them to have the amenities they need. If they are traveling in bigger groups or as a family, it is cheaper to book out an entire place and then prepare meals for themselves. It is also a good idea to book something like this if they are staying for a longer period of time. It can get pretty expensive to eat out or order in every single day. Providing a cooking space allows your guests to cater for themselves, and this brings down the cost of the overall holiday. Not only that, but your guests will be able to enjoy the privacy of having a property to themselves.

One thing to note is that this kind of property will be more expensive than others. You might be limiting your potential guests as single people or couples might not see the need to rent out an entire property. People who are looking to travel around and sightsee might also not want to book out this type of property as they will not be making full use of the amenities.

Private Rooms

A private room still offers privacy but on a budget. A private room will have a bedroom and usually a bathroom that is completely private. Other amenities, such as the living space or kitchen, will be shared with the other guests who stay on the property. If you have a spare room in your house that you are looking to rent out, offering a private room could be a good option. This way, you'll be able to make money from the spare space that you have and create privacy for yourself and your guests. If you are doing this, it might be a good idea to look into creating a separate entrance for your guests so they can come and go as they please, and it's not going to interrupt you and your life.

A private room is a great option for many guests. This is especially so when it is a single person or a couple who is looking to travel. They do not want to stay in their accommodation for long periods as they're looking to be out and about. They are also not too concerned with being able to cook and cater for themselves. Cooking might be an option if there is a communal kitchen available, but this is not necessary for many private room options.

Hotel Rooms

A hotel room offers a level of service that can be likened to traditional hotels. You might find these types of rooms available at lifestyle hotels, boutiques, bed-and-breakfasts, or similar properties. You will be able to charge a bit more for these types of accommodation since you will be offering a service that many other Airbnbs don't. Things like turndown service, breakfast, and cleaning would be expected. It is a great option if you have access to the property that would allow this and you have the funds to provide this or the time to do it yourself.

Shared Rooms

There are many guests who do not mind sharing space with other guests. These tend to be students and travelers who are on a budget. Essentially, you will be able to rent out your space, and the space will be shared amongst many different people. You can think of it more like a hostel or dorm-style room. There might be multiple beds and bunk beds in one room that people sleep in. All amenities on the property will be shared amongst the people who have booked with you.

It is important to note that many travelers might not want to use this option. Families and people who are older generally do not enjoy sharing rooms. However, you are opening up your side of the world to people who want to travel on a budget. This is a great option if you live in a more expensive part of the world that is known for its travel. People want to come to these areas and see them, but they might be on a budget. You'll be offering a place for them to sleep and store their belongings while they go out and see the sights and enjoy the activities.

The pricing for these types of rooms is much less than most other Airbnb options. However, since you will be having a lot more people booking with you since you have more space available, this will offset the cheaper nightly rate. It is likely that the people who book with you would not be staying for long periods of time as they will want to move on to the next destination. This means that the turnover time can be quite quick, and you would need to be ready to clean up and get the rooms ready for the next guest.

Each of the four different types of Airbnb accommodation has its own unique pros and cons when it comes to renting them out. Part of what should drive your decision on which type of listing to launch is also what's in your best financial interest. In the next chapter, we'll compare the profitability of different types of Airbnb listings.

WHAT'S THE MOST PROFITABLE TYPE OF AIRBNB LISTING?

On average, Airbnb guests tend to stay 2.4 times longer in Airbnbs than they do in hotels. This could be attributed to the fact that guests are looking for an experience rather than just a place to sleep at night. If you are able to create a really great place for your guests to stay, you will definitely attract them for a longer period of time and make more money. That being said, there are definitely some properties that are more profitable than others. Understanding which ones can help you make better decisions going forward.

CALCULATING PROFITABILITY

You need to be able to calculate your profitability for your future Airbnb. This will help you to understand how much money you can make with your property.

Key Variables

There are a few key variables that you should take into consideration when you're looking at how profitable your Airbnb could potentially be. Just remember that this is just going to be an estimation. Things might change over the years, so it is a good idea to regularly look at these variables and adjust your expectations accordingly.

Upfront Costs and Operating Expenditures

The first thing you're going to want to look at is the upfront costs and operating expenditures. These are the things that you will continuously be paying for throughout the life of your Airbnb business. This is the general cost of taking care of your property and ensuring that it is at its best. If you already live in the area, you should have a good idea of the maintenance and upkeep costs since you already own a property there. You can use it as a base point and then see if there are any additional costs that you need to include.

You also need to take into account things like taxes, insurance premiums, and platform fees. Your taxes will include property tax and the tax that you make from the profit of your business, so make sure you take both of these into consideration. We will be delving more into insurance in later chapters, but for now, you can just think of this as part of your operating expenditures. The next thing to look at is your platform fees. Every time you get a booking, you will be paying a fee for the platform to process the transaction. This could differ from area to area, so it is important to understand what applies to you.

Occupancy Rates

Your occupancy rate is going to be how often your property is booked out. It is almost impossible to have a 100 percent occupancy rate, so don't feel discouraged if you find that the percentage is lower than what you thought. You are in a good spot if you have around a 50 percent occupancy rate. You can work on increasing this as you see fit. It is pretty easy to work out an occupancy rate; all you need to do is take the days that your property has been booked out and divide that by the number of days it was available to be booked out. You can take this number and multiply it by 100 to get the occupancy rate as a percentage.

So, if your property was booked out for 62 days of the year and there were 120 days available for it to be booked out, your occupancy rate would be 51.7 percent.

62/120 x 100 = 51.7%

When working out your occupancy rate, it is important to take into consideration seasonal fluctuations. There will be times when people are just not going to be traveling as much and other ones where you are going to get an influx of people booking with you. Half of the year, your occupancy rate could be over 70 percent, and the next half could be 30 percent. This is something that you will need to gauge so that you get a good idea of your overall occupancy rate and how much you'll make on an annual basis.

Neighborhood Factors

There are multiple neighborhood factors that can increase or decrease the amount of money that you make through your property. Since Airbnb is a short-term rental service, you need to make sure that whatever area you are going to invest in is going to be best for short-term rentals. Long-term rentals are a completely different thing because people are looking for something different. When people are renting for the long term, they're looking for a place to settle down and be in a good neighborhood. However, this is not the same criteria as for short-term rentals. Short-term rentals are better in areas that provide experiences for the guests or conveniently meet their needs.

There are many tools you can use to help you do a neighborhood analysis. Here are a few that you can consider using:

- AirDNA
- Beyond Pricing
- Host Tools
- Price Labs
- Rate Genie
- Wheelhouse

EXPENSES BY ACCOMMODATION TYPE

Different property types will cost you more or less, depending. You'll need to work out your costs so that you can work out your profit based on the type of property you're looking to invest in. There are definitely pros and cons to the various types of properties you can choose from. It is all up to you, and you need to decide what is going to work best for you. Some of the costs we are going to be speaking about are going to stay the same regardless of the type of property, but most of them will change. You also have to take into consideration your area and other aspects that might impact the price of the listed expenses.

Business License

Certain jurisdictions and areas will require licenses, and you will also pay special taxes in order to run an Airbnb. The cost of these things will vary depending on your state and country. You can have a look at your local laws and regulations to make sure that you understand what you need to pay for and so that you don't incur any unexpected fees down the line.

Property Taxes

These are pretty much unavoidable regardless of where you live. Often, they are included in your mortgage payment, so it is easy to make the required installments. If it is not included in your mortgage, then you will need to make a big once-a-year payment. It is a good idea to save a little bit each month and then pay off your property taxes by the required date. This will make it a lot easier for you to pay, and it won't seem like you are just forking out a whole bunch of money once a year.

Housekeeping and Maintenance

If you are not going to take care of the cleaning and house-keeping yourself, then you'll need to pay somebody to do it. It is usually easier to have somebody come in and clean for you because you will free up time for yourself to work on other aspects of your business or continue working at your regular job. Housekeeping and maintenance are incredibly important because they allow you to get good reviews. Many people over-look how important a clean and well-maintained property is. If you do choose to clean it yourself, you will still need to cover the costs. Include the amount of money you will be spending on cleaning supplies in your expense list.

In terms of maintenance, you will need to put away some money just in case something happens that you need to take care of. If you own your own property, you already know that certain things always pop up. It might be an issue with the plumbing, or the home is in need of a fresh coat of paint. Regardless of what it is, sometimes these matters aren't visible until they actually need to be tended to. This is why it is a good idea to put aside a certain amount of money each month for maintenance costs. When something does happen that needs your attention, you will have the money to deal with it.

Insurance

Insurance is a really important part of running an Airbnb. There are always risks involved, so you need to be sure that you have good insurance and that all the important things are going to be covered.

Goods and Supplies

Typically, you are going to need to provide your guests with a few simple goods and supplies. When your guests live in your home, they are going to use these things. For example, toilet paper, soap, shampoo, coffee, tea, trash bags, and quite a few other disposable things. It would be a good idea for you to buy these things in bulk so that you lower the price of them, and you will always have them on hand so when you are turning over the property for the next guest, you can quickly replace what is needed.

Utilities

Water, gas, trash, sewage, electricity, and Wi-Fi are all important to any kind of rental property. All of those can be quite a big chunk of your expenses, so make sure that you have prepared for them. You don't really have a choice but to pay for these items, and there really isn't much you can do about it, so make sure you have the money available.

Airbnb Fees

Airbnb charges around 3 percent commission on all bookings. Sometimes this can differ based on area, so it is a good idea to check and see. However, you should expect a certain fee to be charged in addition to your booking fee. If you take this into consideration, then you will be able to charge a rate that will offset the fee so that you're not losing too much money.

There are many factors that you need to consider in order to find the most profitable way to rent out your property. You need to think about things like location, the type of property you have, the type of guest that is going to stay at your property, and a number of other things. Taking the time to understand your property and what you will be paying for is a really good way to estimate how much money you will be making from your Airbnb. In the next chapter, we are going to be diving into getting the right insurance for your Airbnb business.

STAGE 2

AIRBNB INSURANCE

AIRBNB INSURANCE—WHICH TYPE OF POLICY SHOULD YOU GET?

If you are just signing up for Airbnb, you might've heard that you can get automatic protection when you activate a listing. Many people believe that because of this, they do not need to get their own insurance. This is not necessarily true. This is why it's important to understand what kind of protection is included in Airbnb's insurance policy.

AIRBNB INSURANCE: WHAT EVERY HOST NEEDS TO KNOW

What exactly is covered by Airbnb AirCover? The main goal of this type of insurance cover is to protect the hosts from damage caused by guests. AirCover is completely free for every Airbnb host who signs up on the platform. Some of the things that are included in this insurance coverage are as follows:

- $1 million in liability insurance
- $3 million in damage protection
- Auto & boat
- Art & valuables
- Pet damage protection
- Deep cleaning protection
- Income loss protection

This may sound amazing, and you might feel pretty secure with this type of offering. However, this does not thoroughly protect your property. It definitely does reduce any out-of-pocket expenses for things like cleaning and damage, but the truth is that it is simply not comprehensive enough to replace regular insurance. In fact, it is not insurance at all. It is simply an alternative to insurance and was created as an incentive to use the platform.

The topic of insurance can be a complicated one, but it is something that you will need to be well versed in if you are going to be in the property business. There are multiple different types of insurance out there, and you need to know which one you should be getting. We are going to go through a few of the different types of insurance out there, and then you can decide which one is going to be the best one for you.

Homeowner's Insurance

Let's first start with homeowner's insurance. If you own a property, then it's very likely that you have this type of insurance. A homeowner's insurance policy will cover damages that are caused by natural disasters and other unforeseen circumstances. Things like fire, lightning, and hail are covered under homeowner's insurance. These things are not covered by Airbnb AirCover, so you can already see the difference here. The issue with homeowner's insurance is that it does not include any kind of business activity. Since most Airbnb hosts do not live at their rental properties, this will apply. If you do live on the property that you are renting out as an Airbnb, then there might be an exception to this, but it is important to check.

If you have homeowner's insurance and are renting out property that you do not stay at, it could be pretty risky. If your insurance company finds out that your home is not used by you and there is some damage that occurs, they will almost always reject your claim. This means that you will have to pay out-of-pocket for all of the damage that has taken place. If you are not living on the property, then homeowner's insurance is simply not going to be enough to cover your property.

Landlord Insurance

The next type of insurance that you can consider is landlord insurance. This includes casualty insurance and property insurance. This protects you, your tenants, and any other employees of the business. The biggest difference between homeowner's and landlord insurance is that the landlord insurance will offer income protection. What this means is that if your home is not fit for renters due to an unforeseen circumstance, like a natural disaster, your insurance policy will pay you your rental income. Landlord insurance does not cover things that are personal to your property, such as furniture, art, and appliances.

You will need to have a conversation with your insurance provider because many landlord insurance policies don't actually cover short-term rentals. If you are planning on renting out your Airbnb for more than a month, then landlord insurance could be a good option for you, but if it's less than 30 days, it's not going to be of many benefits. However, you can consider something like home-sharing insurance if you are just renting out one of your rooms on the property while you are still living in the main house.

Commercial Property Insurance

Commercial, home-sharing, or vacation rental policies are good options if you are choosing to rent out your property as a true Airbnb with consecutive short-term guests. A commercial property policy is also known as a business property policy. This is definitely one of the most common options. If you do not live on your property and are only using it for short-term rentals, it is possibly your best option. This type of insurance will cover liability and property. This means that damage to your property or any damage or injuries that happen to your guests will all be covered.

Umbrella Policies

An umbrella policy is simply an extension of liability coverage that is typically offered in homeowner's or landlord policies. These will reimburse you for any damages incurred above what has been outlined in the underlying policy. For example, if one of your guests gets injured due to a fault on the property and then decides to sue you, your homeowner's or landlord insurance will pay the initial claim. Anything over and above that will be covered by the umbrella policy. A blanket umbrella possibly covers properties in multiple cities or states. This makes it a really good option for any Airbnb investor who has properties in more than one place. You should make sure that you understand what will be covered by your umbrella policy and how it will all work. Not all of them will work exactly the same, so doing research is of the utmost importance.

There are definitely many things to consider when you are choosing an insurance policy for your Airbnb business. Although you will automatically get AirCover, it only provides certain types of protection for the host. This is simply not enough and should be supplemented with additional insurance coverage. In the next chapter, we will discuss some practical safety tips you can apply as an Airbnb host to help minimize any damage incurred.

SAFETY TIPS FOR HOSTS

While you might've heard that it can be dangerous for guests, the truth is that less than 0.1 percent of all stays result in serious safety issues.[1] This is quite a small statistic, so is it something to worry about? The truth is, it is the host's responsibility to make sure that nothing bad happens to the guest. Even though there is a very small chance that anything will happen, it is good to be prepared and make sure that you put in place the best safety practices that you can.

MOST COMMON PROBLEMS THAT HOSTS FACE

There can definitely be some unexpected situations that pop up when you are a host. However, you can prepare for the most common ones so that you're not completely caught off guard if they do happen.

Payment Disputes

Payment disputes tend to be quite common when you are renting out your property to short-term visitors. However, when you're using the Airbnb platform, these are not things that you would typically have to worry about. Since all payments are handled through the platform, it is a lot safer than dealing one-on-one with the customer. Both the guest and the host are protected in terms of payments.

Physical Injuries to Guests

If a guest gets injured on your property due to negligence or there is an issue with a facility that is on your property, they can sue you. This is why it is so important to have insurance to cover this and to make sure that your property is safe. Doing an inspection of your property every few months will help minimize the risk of this happening.

Theft of Personal Belongings or High-Valued Possessions

As much as you would like to believe that everybody who stays on your property is going to take care of your possessions and not steal them, this is definitely something that can happen. It's a risk you take when you are an Airbnb host. This is why it's best to not leave any kind of high-value possessions or personal belongings at the rental property. Do your best to ensure that anything that you deem valuable is not going to be there. This way, you can have peace of mind when your guests stay with you. Insurance usually covers theft and loss of belongings, but make sure that your insurance policy does include this.

Property Damage

Property damage is also a common risk that you have to think about. If you have a good insurance policy, then this will be covered. It is important to screen your guests as best as possible to make sure that they are responsible. With this being said, there really is only so much that you find out about your guests. There will always be a risk of property damage when other people are using your facilities.

BEST SAFETY PRACTICES FOR AIRBNB HOSTS

Even though there are plenty of risks that come with renting out your property to strangers, there are things that you can do to keep yourself and your property safe. If you stick to these safety practices, then you will significantly minimize the risk of having to deal with any unfortunate situations.

Only Interact Using Airbnb's Platform

It might seem beneficial to take all your business dealings off the platform because you would be able to skip the Airbnb fee and do things the way you want to. However, this is typically not the best idea because it can leave you vulnerable to certain situations. The platform has been designed in such a way as to protect both the guest and the host. When a guest puts in a request to book certain dates, you have the opportunity to look at their profile and find out more about them. If you take things off the platform, you do not have access to profiles, reviews, or references. Everything is simply left to chance.

Be Clear with House Rules, House Manual, and Expectations

The Airbnb platform will allow a host to create a house manual and rules and then upload them. This is completely visible to the guests, so they know what is going to be expected of them if they stay with you. This allows you to hold your guests accountable to the expectations that you set. You know that they have access to the rules and manual, so there really isn't an excuse for them to misuse any of your items. You can put in any type of rule that you deem fit. Your rules can include things like smoking, quiet hours, wearing shoes in the house, or Wi-Fi usage.

Even though setting these rules is really important, you have to be mindful of not overdoing them. If you set unnecessary rules, then people are going to be turned off from booking with you. At the end of the day, people still want to enjoy their holiday, and they don't want to be thinking about whether or not they can do certain things at home. You still want to make them feel comfortable and welcome in your home, but set a few guide-lines so that it protects you both.

Have the Right Insurance

As you already know, insurance is of the utmost importance. Make sure that you do thorough research and get the right insurance for you. It is also a good idea to shop around for insurance. You don't want to pay more than you actually need to because insurance can be a costly expense. If you compare quotes from various insurers, then you can be sure that you are getting the best deal and the best coverage.

Get a Security Deposit for Every Stay

It is definitely in your best interest to ask for a security deposit from your guests. In the event of some minor damage, you will be able to dip into the security deposit and pay for it. Some damages don't really warrant an insurance claim, so collecting a security deposit means that you are not going to be expected to foot the bill for damages that were caused by the carelessness of the guest. If there was no damage, then the guest gets the security deposit back. Doing this actually helps keep the guest accountable because they want to get their money back, so they aren't going to be as careless.

Have a Security System Installed

A security system is a great investment for both your protection and that of your guests. You will be able to protect your home even when you are not there. It also helps you to keep tabs on everything that is going on. You will be able to automate things like the thermostat, locking up the doors, and the lights. One thing to note is that you will not be able to install security cameras in certain places that would be considered to be an invasion of your guests' privacy. If there are cameras on the outside of the property, then make sure you have notified your guests about this and understand the laws that surround things like this.

Add Smoke and Carbon Monoxide Detectors

Adding these two things helps give your guests peace of mind, and it also protects your property investment. It really doesn't cost that much to buy and install them, so it's not going to put you out a lot of money. You'll be able to add these features to your listings so that it builds trust and shows your guests that you take their safety seriously. You should test these detectors often so you can ensure they are still working properly.

Use Proper Cybersecurity Measures

There are risks from cyberattacks, and many people do not think of this. Home network security devices will alert you of any threats or Wi-Fi attacks. You will also be able to set a limit on how many people can connect to the device. This means that if your guests invite more people to your home and connect them to your Wi-Fi, you will be able to keep tabs on them.

You can also consider getting a VPN router that does not track your online activity. This means anything your guests do will remain private and cannot be traced back to your home's Wi-Fi. This means that you will not be held liable for any of their actions. This creates privacy for them and protection for you.

Even though insurance is really important, you do not want to be put in a position where you have to use it all the time. Insurance claims can be tiresome, and property damage will cause a lot of hassle for you. This is why you need to put things in place to prevent this from happening in the first place. If you do everything in your power to ensure that your property is safe and that you've created a safe environment for your guests, then you will likely not have to deal with insurance companies very often. In the next chapter, we are going to be looking at things that need to be done before you can list your property on Airbnb.

STAGE 3

READYING YOUR PROPERTY

THE ULTIMATE CHECKLIST FOR ITEMS TO BUY FOR YOUR PROPERTY

New hosts that joined Airbnb since the start of the pandemic have collectively earned over $1 billion.[1] This is just the new hosts, so as you can see, it has been quite profitable even throughout a time when people traveled at a limited capacity. This being said, you need to ensure that you have everything in place in order to cater to your guests' needs. Creating checklists is going to help you in this regard. It allows you to keep tabs on what you need to provide your guests and what has run out. This ensures that you're not missing out on anything and that every guest will get the same experience.

BATHROOM(S)

- Bath Towels
- Hand Towels

- Toilet Paper
- Hand Soap
- Shampoo
- Conditioner
- Body Wash
- Toothpaste
- Floss
- Additional Toiletries
- Body Lotion
- Disposable Razors
- Disposable Toothbrushes
- Shower Caddy
- Towel Rack
- Hair Dryer
- Bath Mat
- Plunger
- Garbage Can

BEDROOM(S)

- Bed Linens
- Pillows
- Tissues
- Safe for Valuables
- Bedside Table and Lamp
- Garbage Can
- Notepad and Pen
- Hangers for Clothing
- Alarm Clock

KITCHEN

- Tea and Coffee
- Tea Kettle
- Sugar and Spices
- Dishes
- Pots and Pans
- Silverware
- Cups
- Wine Glasses
- Ice Trays
- Coasters
- Tupperware
- Cleaning Supplies
- Dishwashing Liquid
- Hand Soap
- Trash Bags
- Mop
- Broom
- Dustpan
- Oven Mitts
- Dish Towels

LIVING ROOM

- Coffee Table Reading Items (Books, Magazines, Travel Guides)
- Pens and Pencils

APPLIANCES

- Washer and Dryer
- Television
- Cable and/or Subscription Streaming Service
- Clothing Iron and Ironing Board
- Wi-Fi

SAFETY EQUIPMENT

- First Aid Kit
- Smoke Alarm and Carbon Monoxide Detector
- Fire Extinguisher
- Contact List for Emergency Services
- Wi-Fi Thermostat
- Childproofing
- Disaster Kit
- Anti-slip Mats

CLEANING SUPPLIES AND EQUIPMENT

- Cleaning Spray
- Paper Towels
- Gloves
- Duster
- Powdered Cleanser
- Magic Eraser
- Drain Cleaner

- Broom and Dustpan
- Vacuum

When it comes to listing your property on Airbnb, the small details really do matter. These are the things that will help you get those 5-star reviews. Creating a list and structure for yourself will make sure that you're not letting any of these things slip or fall through the cracks. In the next chapter, we are going to go over how to establish effective house rules so that you can ensure the safety of your property and your guests.

TOP 10 TIPS FOR ESTABLISHING EFFECTIVE HOUSE RULES

One of the easiest ways to keep yourself from getting into heated disputes with the guests is to set clear expectations from the start. In order to do this, you can utilize house rules. This will make sure that your guests understand exactly what you expect from them, and you can hold them accountable if they do not follow the rules.

WHAT ARE AIRBNB'S HOUSE RULES?

Your house rules are exactly what they sound like. You'll be setting rules for your guests to adhere to during their stay. This sets expectations and prevents misunderstandings. It also allows you to hold guests accountable for anything that happens. There are already some built-in house rules that are on the Airbnb platform. You can go through these and then add to them to ensure that you are covering all your bases. Some house rules are going to be specific to your type of property, while others are just going to be about general aspects of rental properties.

TOP TIPS FOR SETTING HOUSE RULES

Well-structured house rules allow both parties to understand what is to be expected. The goal is to make your rules clear and understandable for your guests. This will minimize any miscommunications and misunderstandings.

Tip #1: Be Specific and Clear

The first tip is to be specific and clear. You want to make sure that there is no room for misinterpretation. Even if it means that you have to use very simple language, try not to use any big words or unnecessary language, as this can confuse guests. You have to take into consideration that many people who are staying on your Airbnb might not be native English speakers or might not know the local terms that you use. This is why it's so important to be as simple as possible so that your rules are as clear as possible.

Tip #2: Be Reasonable

It can be very easy to go overboard with these rules. Please remember that you want guests to have fun and not feel like they are being extremely restricted. This is why it's so important to be reasonable with the rules that you set. Think about your guests' experience when you are setting the rules. Guests will look at the rules before they book, and if you have too many restrictions, they might not want to book with you. It might be a good idea to have a friend or family member look over your rules and give their opinion on them. This way, you can get an outside view of it and tweak it from there.

Tip #3: Tailor Your Rules to Your Target Guest

When you're writing your rules, take into consideration your target guest. You need to make sure that the rules are relevant to them. Try and read your rules from the point of view of your target guest. Think about whether you would appreciate all the rules or points given to you if you were in their shoes. You can remove all the irrelevant points and change your language based on who your guest is. This will help you communicate better with them and make sure that your rules are actually relevant.

Tip #4: Keep It Friendly

While it is important to be extremely clear with your rules, it is advisable to be friendly and polite as well. You don't want to come off as demanding and rude. All guests would like to be treated nicely and not be spoken to as children. Check the tone in which your rules are coming across. You can write it in a commanding tone, but remember not to be arrogant. In order to do this, you can add a few friendly touches here and there. You can add a few lines before the start of the rules list to set a friendly tone for what is to come. A guest should feel pretty comfortable when they read the rules, but also understand how important it is to do so.

Tip #5: Communicate Your House Rules Early On

From as early on as possible, make sure that your guests understand and respect the house rules. You can make it very easy for your guests to view your house rules even before they book. Once they have booked, you can email them a list of the rules along with the other information that you want to give them. Another helpful tip is to have a list of the house rules in your welcome package when the guests arrive. All of these will solidify the rules in your guests' heads and make sure that they aren't missing anything. They will already know what you expect of them before they get to your property and will be reminded of it at various intervals.

Tip #6: Keep It Concise

Once you've decided on all the important points of your house rules, you need to make sure that it's not too long and tedious to read. Each rule should be short and not consist of more than around ten words. This will allow your guests to quickly move through the rules and not feel like there's too much information to take in. Stick to one sentence for each rule. For example, instead of saying, "we highly encourage that you do not smoke on our premises as this can lead to an unpleasant experience for the next guests who arrive," you can simply say, "no smoking allowed." It is short and simple, and it gets your message across with no miscommunication.

Tip #7: Use Bullet Points

Bullet points are your friends. Bullet points make things a lot easier to read. When everything is in one long paragraph, it can be difficult for your guests to move through it. Bullet points will allow your guests to skim through the rules at a quick pace, and it just seems a lot more inviting and easier to read. It also helps them see how many rules there are at your property.

Tip #8: Prioritize Your Rules in Order of Importance

When you are creating a list of rules for your guests, make sure that they are in order of importance. As your guests read through the list, it is pretty likely that they will get bored by the time they come to the end. This is why, if you have the most important ones at the beginning, you know that these are definitely going to be the ones that are followed and taken notice of.

Tip #9: Have Your Rules Online and at the Property

Make sure your guests can access your rules online and have a physical copy at your property. If the rules are online, your guests will know what is expected of them before they get to the property. They will also be able to ask you any questions they might have about the rules. Then you can create a physical reminder for them if you have this printed out and at the property. This way, it is easy for them to have a look at them when they need to.

Tip #10: Use an Appropriate Structure

When you are writing out your rules list, make sure that you have structured it in a way that is easy for them to read and understand. You can create a poster with all the rules on it so that it is easy to understand. Feel free to add visuals to the printed copies of your rules so that they are more eye-catching and not dull. The main point about these rules is that they are easy to understand for your guests.

Establishing house rules is an important part of not only building a solid relationship with your guests but also automating your Airbnb business, so you have fewer problems to deal with in the future. It is one of the most important things you can do when you are renting out your property. In the next chapter, we'll look at using your house rules to create your house manual.

HOW TO CREATE YOUR HOUSE MANUAL

A simple key to setting yourself apart from other Airbnb hosts and delivering a memorable experience for your guests is providing a comprehensive house manual that thoroughly details your home. House manuals should be easy to access for your guests and provide easy-to-use instructions for everything they need. You can guarantee that your guests will have a much better experience when they understand how to use everything available on the property.

WHAT IS A HOUSE MANUAL?

You might be thinking that you do not have to create a manual because you already have the house rules. However, the house manual is something a bit different. It is basically like a how-to guide for your home. There might be things in your home that need a bit more explanation in order for your guests to understand how to use them. It will allow your guests to have a reference guide if they encounter any problems during their stay.

The house rules are basically like the do's and don'ts of your home, but the house manual shows your guests how to use things properly. You can add things to your house manual, such as how to use certain appliances, where to find amenities, and how the guests can make the most of their stay with you. The content and purpose of house rules versus house manuals are completely different. Your house manual does not show up on your Airbnb listing page. Instead, you will leave a copy of your house manual in the home when your guest checks in, and you can send a copy to them once the reservation has been confirmed.

WHAT DOES A HOUSE MANUAL LOOK LIKE?

There are many different formats in which you can structure your house manual. It really doesn't have to be rocket science, and you can definitely show your personality through it. The first thing that you're going to need is a short welcome message. This is a personal welcome message that you will write in order to establish a connection with your guests. This is especially important if you are not meeting your guests at check-in. Remember not to go overboard with your welcome message. Short and sweet is typically best. Here is an example of a good welcome message:

Dear Guest,

Welcome to [insert house name here]. We are so excited to have you stay with us!

This home is incredibly special to us, and we have made so many memories in it. We hope that you will be able to create many amazing memories as well.

Over the past few years, we have really enjoyed renting it out to travelers such as yourself. This home is a great starting point to discover the city and its surroundings. There is so much to do and see, and I'm sure you will fall in love with the city just as we have.

In this manual, you will find tons of important information. This will help you to make the most of your stay. There are instructions on how to use appliances, recommendations for delicious food places, and much more.

We truly hope that you have a magical stay!

Sincerely,

[Insert your name]

As you can see, this welcome note is personal and welcoming. It seems very friendly and shows the guest that there is a person behind the rental property. It also isn't long or drawn out because most of the information is going to be in the manual anyway.

After the welcome message, you can include some property information as well as contact information. This will be your contact info, emergency contact details, and if you are using a property manager, then include their contact details as well. You can also include the Wi-Fi password and any other codes or passwords they would need in order to utilize things in your house. This can be just after the first page so that it's easy to find.

You can attach your house rules to your manual so that everything is in one place. Then you give a general walk-through of your property's essentials. This can be how to use the various appliances so your guests understand how to operate everything in a way that is safe. This will prevent your guests from breaking anything because they are confused or simply don't understand certain aspects of your home. Even if you think it is common sense, it is really best to have these instructions. If your guests are coming from other countries, it is likely that they would do things differently and might not have the same types of appliances as you.

Other important details that you should include are check-in and check-out times. This is just a reminder because they should already know the times beforehand. If you provide parking for your guests, then include some parking information and instructions. This will prevent them from parking in a spot that obstructs other vehicles and people who live in your area. Also, include some local transport information so your guests can easily get around town. This is especially important if they are not arriving in their own car.

A page with some information about the local area is always welcome. You are the expert on the city or area in which your guests are staying. You want to ensure that they are going to have a good time, so give them a few recommendations for amazing restaurants, sightseeing spots, or local treasures. There might be things you know that are not common knowledge, and you can share this with your guests so they have a good experience and stories to tell.

You should also include an emergency page. This page will have emergency contact details for the local services around you. The fire department, police station, and other emergency services are important. It is highly unlikely that your guests would need to use these emergency services, but it is a good idea to have this information. You can also include information as to where the fire extinguisher and first aid kits are. This should be the last page of your manual, as this will make it easier for your guests to find if they do need it.

Even though this might seem like a lot of information, it really isn't. When you are structuring your manual, you will see that the information doesn't fill more than a few pages. When we think of manuals, we can think of thick books, but this should not be the case. Your guests are not going to be reading through a hundred-page document when they are on vacation. Your manual should not be more than a few pages long and just cover the necessities.

A house manual is like a comprehensive guide for living in your home. Making a detailed house manual goes a long way to helping form a clear understanding of the expectations between guests and hosts. It also allows the guest to understand how to utilize the property correctly so they have the best stay possible. In the next chapter, we will be going through legal and compliance issues you may have to consider before starting your own Airbnb business.

LEGAL REGULATIONS TO CONSIDER

The average host in the US earns the highest in the world per year, at over $18,000 annually.[1] In most cities and states, it is going to be easy for the average US citizen to take part in Airbnb. However, it is important to understand the legal regulations so that you don't have to pay any penalties or fees later on. This helps you to be better prepared and understand what your government requires from you in order to start an Airbnb business.

COMMON LEGAL RESTRICTIONS RELATED TO AIRBNB

When you are an Airbnb host, it is really important that you understand the laws in your city, country, state, or territory. The platform doesn't actually provide any legal advice, so it is a good idea to get this advice directly from your government or municipality. However, there are some considerations that could help you to understand the laws and regulations in your jurisdiction.

Business Licenses

There are many jurisdictions that require business owners or operators to apply for a license. You will need to do this before you can start operating your business. You will be able to find up-to-date information on this on your local government website. Most government websites have sections explaining the business licensing process and provide you with all the forms and relevant information that you will need.

Building Codes

Most governments have certain rules and regulations that specify minimum construction, design, and maintenance standards for buildings. These can also include health, safety, and habitability regulations. There are also certain rules that will apply to residential and non-residential uses of a property. Furthermore, certain jurisdictions might require that you take part in an inspection to make sure that your property meets the minimum requirements and standards. Only then will you be able to utilize your property as an Airbnb. Not all jurisdictions or areas will have such strict rules, so it is important to know what applies to you by going on the government website or contacting your local government.

Zoning Rules

There could be many rules or laws that dictate how you use your home. These can be found in a zoning code, city ordinance, or planning code. You can consult these rules and regulations to find out if your listing is consistent with the current requirements or uses definitions.

Special Permits

You might be required to get a special permit in order to rent out your home. You'll need to contact your local government or municipality to see if this applies to you. You will also be able to get some information on how you can get this permit.

Tax Laws

Most states and jurisdictions will require an Airbnb host to collect tax for each stay. You will then need to pay this tax to the city or to the jurisdiction where it applies. There are certain jurisdictions where Airbnb will automatically collect and remit certain taxes on your behalf. You will need to find out if this applies to you so that you have the relevant tax information.

Landlord-Tenant Laws

If you are hosting longer stays, you might be subject to landlord-tenant laws. This varies by jurisdiction and may impose more strict legal obligations on you and provide your guests with additional legal rights. It is a good idea to consult a lawyer that specializes in landlord-tenant law in order to learn more and see what applies to you.

WHERE TO LOOK FOR APPLICABLE LAWS AND REGULATIONS

The laws and regulations can seem a bit confusing, but it is quite easy to get the information that you need in order to make the right decisions going forward. You can log on to the Airbnb help center and see what kind of regulations apply to your city. This might not provide all the information you need, but it can provide a guideline.

If you are in North America, then you will most likely be required to obtain permits and business licenses before you can operate your Airbnb. The exact requirements will vary depending on many different factors. You can start off by going onto your local government website to see what kind of permits or licenses you would need in order to start a short-term rental business. In most cases, you will find a comprehensive guide and the steps that you need to take in order to obtain the permits. You would likely be able to fill out all the forms you need online and then submit them. If you are confused, you can call your government offices and see if they can help you with any of your queries.

Once you have determined exactly what permits and documents you need in order to start your business, you need to make sure that your property is in compliance. Each location will have its own safety regulations for the tenants. If you need to make any renovations or improvements to your property, then do so. Also, obtain proper insurance to ensure your guests' and your safety. You will also need to make sure that you comply with any requirements your insurance company might have in order to insure you for certain things.

It is so important that you consult your local laws and rules to make sure that you are not violating any regulations when you start an Airbnb. It is better to seek clarification and ask as many questions as possible, rather than assume that everything is going to be fine in the end. You don't want to be struck down with heavy fines, end up being sued, or possibly end up being evicted just because of a technicality that could have been avoided. Rather, do all the necessary homework now so that you can avoid any unpleasant situations in the future. In the next chapter, we are going to be talking about keeping your property clean and well-maintained in order to get those 5-star reviews.

A CLEAN PROPERTY LEADS TO 5-STAR REVIEWS

Many negative reviews come from the fact that the property has not been cleaned properly or is unkempt and untidy. Your guests might stay at an amazing property with beautiful amenities, but if it is not clean, they are going to complain. Would you like to stay in a hotel or guest house that is not clean? We all have higher standards of cleanliness when we are paying for a vacation rental. This means that you have to put a lot of emphasis on making sure your property is clean and neat.

TURNING OVER YOUR PROPERTY

Cleaning your property between stays is called turning over the property. It is not just about doing a quick clean and then welcoming the next guest. When your guests check in, you want them to feel that they are in an absolutely pristine boutique hotel. When you are doing a turnover cleaning, it is going to require a bit more energy and work than a regular house cleaning. It is a good idea to clean up your property as soon as your guest leaves. This will allow you time to discover if there are any damages or problems so you can process a claim as soon as possible. If there are any damaged items or items that need to be replaced, you have time to do this before the next guest arrives.

Turning over your property requires consistency. You need to create a system for yourself so that each guest gets the exact same experience. This actually makes it a lot easier, and you'll find that you can turn over your property a lot quicker as time goes on. It's a good idea to use a checklist so that you understand what needs to be cleaned and you don't miss anything. Later on in this chapter, we are going to give you an example of a checklist that you can use and tweak depending on your property.

Many first-time hosts underestimate the amount of time they need to clean their property. Of course, the size of your property definitely comes into play when it comes to how long you will spend cleaning. When your guests check out, you will only have a specific amount of time in order to clean it and get it ready for the next guest. You should have at least a four- or five-hour cleaning window so that you can do things thoroughly and make sure that everything is up to standard.

You might have to consider hiring a cleaner if you are not going to be available to turn over the property or if the work is going to be too much for you to handle on your own. If you are going to hire a professional team, make sure that you have cleaned your own property before and know exactly what needs to be done. This allows you to set the standard so you can communicate effectively with your team about what they need to get done. You will then need to provide them with a checklist as well so that the standard remains consistent.

It is also important that you do a thorough inspection when you are turning over the property. A guest might have broken something, or there might have been some sort of malfunction.

It is a good idea to test all the appliances and the plug points to make sure that everything is still working fine. Also, check through the glassware and other commonly used items to make sure that nothing is chipped or broken. It is a good idea to bring a few extras with you when you come to turn over your property. You will need to replace anything that is broken so that the next guest gets a good experience.

REMEMBER TO RESTOCK AND RESTAGE

The turnover time also needs to include restocking and restaging your property. As your guests use your property, things are going to be moved around and finished. You need to make sure that you have reverted the property back to default settings so that your next guests are able to enjoy it just the same. Using the checklist that was given to you in Chapter 11 is a great starting point. Make sure that you bring all the items that could be used up with you. Things like toilet paper, shampoo, conditioner, tissues, and pantry items, will all need to be replaced. If you have these with you, then it's going to make it a lot easier for you to simply replace them. You can take any extras back to your storage.

Restaging simply means moving all the furniture and other items back to how they were before your guests checked in. It is a good idea to take a few pictures of your ideal property setting. This way, you can use the picture as a reference when you are moving everything back. It'll make things a lot easier until you are used to restaging your property. When you are cleaning, it is going to be a good idea to move the furniture so you can get underneath, just in case your guests have dropped things or lost things under the furniture. Then you can move things back into the ideal position.

Have a look at your decor items and make sure that they are all clean and in the proper position. When guests stay at a property, they might move things like artwork, decor, and similar items. You can simply wipe them down and move them back to where they are supposed to be. Since you are restaging for the next guest, candles are a good idea to add some ambiance to your property. Check to see that all the candles are not completely burned down or finished. You can replace them as needed. If you have any other disposable decor items, then you can also replace these and make sure that they are in the right position.

Your guests are going to expect the property to look like the listing photos. This is why it is so important to make sure that you are resetting your property to how it was in those photos. If you have cleaners that are working for you, then make sure they have access to these photos so they have a reference to how the furniture and settings should look.

Your guests' welcome package is something that you're going to have to restock every time. You can actually create a few welcome packages and keep them with you. This way you can just replace the old ones each time you turn over the property. You can provide these to your cleaners and your property managers so they can do the same for you.

CREATE A CHECKLIST

A checklist is really helpful to make sure that you are providing each guest with the exact same service. Here is an example of a housekeeping and turnover checklist that you can use on your own Airbnb.

Kitchen:

- Wash and put away the dishes.
- Wipe and sanitize all surfaces.
- Wipe and disinfect sink and backsplash.
- Clean inside and outside of fridge, freezer, and oven.
- Wipe down all small appliances like coffee maker and microwave.
- Refill all kitchen cleaning supplies like dish soap and sponges.

- Clean windows and dust the windowsills.
- Mop the floor.
- Take out trash, clean the garbage can, and put a fresh trash bag in.
- Ensure all kitchen supplies are arranged nicely.

Bedrooms:

- Remove sheets, pillowcases, blankets, and mattress protectors. Make sure they are laundered properly.
- Wipe down all surfaces including ceiling fans and decor.
- Remove smudges from windows and mirrors.
- Disinfect high-touch items like remotes and light switches.
- Check for any personal belongings that have been left behind.
- Check for damage on furniture and bedding.
- Vacuum the floors.
- Empty trash cans.
- Restock with fresh linen.
- Remake the bed with a clean and fresh set of bedding.
- Arrange all decor and artwork correctly.

Bathrooms:

- Remove all dirty towels and bath mats; have them laundered correctly.
- Look in the drawers and cabinets for any personal items left behind.

- Wipe down mirrors and windows.
- Disinfect countertops, sinks, faucets, and backsplashes.
- Scrub down the bathtubs and showers.
- Clean and sanitize the toilets thoroughly.
- Dust all windowsills, fans, and vents.
- Sweep and mop the floors.
- Replace and refill all amenities such as hand soap and toilet paper.
- Check bathroom for signs of wear and tear and damage.
- Place clean towels and bathmats appropriately.
- Ensure all the bathroom items are arranged neatly.

Living Room:

- Wipe down all tables, shelving, and furniture.
- Dust appliances such as the TV and radio, as well as decor.
- Wipe down windows, doors, and windowsills.
- Dust lighting fixtures such as lamps and ceiling fans.
- Sanitize frequently touched items like light switches and remotes.
- Wipe down and refresh couches, throw pillows, and chairs.
- Launder any blankets and replace them with new ones.
- Sweep and mop or vacuum the floors and carpets.
- Ensure any additional items such as books, board games, decor, or art are arranged neatly.
- Arrange throw pillows and blankets neatly on the couch.

Dining Room:

- Wipe down tables and chairs; make sure there are no crumbs in any hard-to-reach places.
- Check underneath table to make sure there is nothing stuck underneath it.
- Wash tablecloths and runners.
- Clean centerpieces.
- Wipe down all decor and replace in appropriate areas.

Outdoor Areas:

- Remove any branches and dead leaves from the lawn.
- Ensure all the bushes are trimmed and neat.
- Remove any debris or weeds.
- Wipe down all outdoor furniture.
- Clean railings.
- Sweep the patio or deck.

Laundry:

- Check for clothes left behind in the washing machine or dryer.
- Clean out any washing detergent left in the washing machine compartment.
- Wipe down all surfaces.

It is so important that you take the time to turn over your property correctly. If you have a look through Airbnb reviews, you will see that one of the most common things that people complain about is cleanliness. You can easily get marked down two or three points just because your property is not clean. In chapter 16, we will be moving on to setting up your booking system.

YOUR SECRET SUPERPOWER AS AN AIRBNB OWNER

If you have knowledge, let others light their candles in it.

— MARGARET FULLER

In Chapter 25, we're going to look at the power of good reviews – and how you can get them. Think back to the last time you booked travel accommodation for yourself. I'd hazard a guess that reviews are one of the first things you looked at. Although we'll delve into this in more detail later on, it's worth having in the back of your mind at all times that positive reviews are your secret superpower as an Airbnb owner... which is why I'm planting this seed in your mind now.

Your property is a place people want to feel safe and comfortable while they're away from home, so it's clear that reviews are going to be very important for you. They let other travelers know exactly what they're getting for their money, what their experience will be like, and ultimately, whether they're making the right choice for them. Positive reviews give customers faith in your property and influence their decision to book.

I want to help other business owners like you because I truly believe Airbnb can be a lucrative and fulfilling business for anyone – and reviews are just as important for authors as they are for business owners. So, as you might have guessed by now, I'd like to ask for your help.

Simply by leaving your honest review of this book on Amazon, you can help the Airbnb business remain the gold-mine it is today.

Just as reviews tell guests which property is right for them, they tell readers which books will provide them with the information they need. As a result, more business owners like you will see success... and *that's* how Airbnb will remain the lucrative business it is today, serving you and your fellow hosts well into the future.

Thank you for taking the time to help me here – and I hope it illustrates just how important those reviews are going to be for you. Keep reading to find out more!

Scan this QR code and leave a brief review on Amazon.

STAGE 4

SETTING UP AND MANAGING BOOKINGS

BOOKING POLICIES TO CONSIDER

B efore you can even think about creating your listing on Airbnb, it is important to give some thought to the policies you want to enforce for guests staying on the property. Thinking about these things before actually publishing your listing helps you to be prepared, and eliminates any unnecessary issues down the line. Prevention of problems is always better when it comes to dealing with other people. This will be a lot less stressful for you and your guests. It will also help your guests to understand exactly what is expected from them.

COMMON BOOKING POLICIES THAT GUESTS ASK ABOUT

When you're running a short-term rental property, there are a few booking policies that guests are going to be concerned about. The Airbnb platform allows space for you to communicate what your booking policies are like so that it is clear and your guests understand it from the get-go.

Cancellation Policy

The first kind of policy that we are going to be talking about is the cancellation policy. It is also arguably one of the most important policies that you should think about. The Airbnb platform gives you a few options to choose from, and this is all going to be based on your preferences and what you deem as the best fit for you. These are the most commonly used policies.

Flexible Cancellation

The flexible cancellation policy allows your guests to cancel their booking and get a full refund up until 24 hours prior to check-in. In that case, you won't get paid. If they cancel after that, you will be paid for every night they stay plus one additional night.

Many guests like the flexible cancellation policy because it allows them to get a full refund. With this being said, it might not benefit you as it is difficult to find somebody who wants to book in their place within a day. When the cancellation can be done so close to the actual check-in time, it might result in you losing money. This is definitely something to think about when you are renting out your Airbnb.

Moderate Cancellation

A moderate cancellation policy allows the guest to cancel the booking and get a full refund up to 5 days before check-in. If the guest cancels after this, you will be paid for every night they do stay plus an additional night. You will also get 50 percent for all unspent nights. Using this kind of cancellation policy allows you to have a bit more security and it holds the guest a bit more accountable. They will not be able to cancel and get a full refund unless they cancel at least 5 days in advance. This might give you some extra time to find someone else to book in their place and still make money.

Strict Cancellation

A strict cancellation policy will allow your guests to receive a full refund if they cancel within the first 48 hours after they have made the booking. This needs to be at least 14 days prior to check-in. If the guest cancels between 7 and 14 days before check-in they will receive a 50 percent refund on the nightly rate, but will not be refunded for the service fee. If they cancel within 7 days of arrival, there is no refund. A strict cancellation policy means that if a guest books with you, they need to be sure that they can stick to the commitment. The issue with this type of policy is that it can put a lot of guests off. They might not want to book too far in advance just in case they have to cancel, and this means they would be looking for another property that would be a bit more flexible.

If you are new to running your own Airbnb, then it might not be a good idea to have this kind of cancellation policy. Since you have not yet built up your reputation and probably don't have that many reviews, there is no guarantee for your guests that your property is going to be worth it. As you build up your reputation and more people start to know you and your property, it would be a better time to implement this kind of cancellation policy. Properties that are very popular and have back-to-back bookings tend to do better with this kind of cancellation policy because people will do their best to ensure that they get a spot and keep the commitment to this day.

Flexible Long-Term Cancellation

If you are going to rent out your property on a long-term basis, 28 days or longer, it overrides the standard cancellation policy. The guest would need to cancel 30 days prior to check-in in order to receive a full refund. If they cancel after this time has elapsed, you will receive full payment for the nights they stay and for an additional 30 nights. If fewer than 30 days remain on the initial reservation, you will be paid for all remaining nights. This is done to protect you, as a host, since you will find it very difficult to find a new guest for a long-term stay in a short period of time.

Super Strict Cancellation

The super strict policy is not available to every host. Only experienced hosts who Airbnb has invited can select this option. There are also two options: super strict for 30 days and super strict for 60 days. The 30-day option means that if a guest cancels at least 30 days before check-in they will receive 50 percent of the total nightly rate. The service fee is non-refundable. If you choose the 60-day option, the guest would need to cancel 60 days before check-in to receive a 50 percent refund on the total nightly rate. The service fee for this option is also not refundable.

Non-refundable Option

If you are concerned about guests canceling their booking, you can set up a non-refundable policy. To do this, you would need to offer a discount of 10% off your base rate. Guests can then choose under which policy they book with you. If they choose the discounted rate, the booking will be non-refundable, and in case of a cancellation, you will get paid for all nights booked. The reservation will be subject to your cancellation policy if they choose the standard rate.

Cleaning Fees

There is an option to add a cleaning fee on top of your regular nightly rate. This helps with expenses that will go toward the maintenance and upkeep of the property. Guests will see the total that will include the cleaning fee as they browse through the site. When they get the bill, the fees will be listed separately, so your guests will know exactly what they are paying for. Bear in mind that if the cleaning fee brings up the total nightly stay price significantly, this might deter a few guests from wanting to stay with you.

Security Deposit

Airbnb will not charge a security deposit. Instead, Airbnb will inform every guest at the time of booking that they may be charged if they cause any damage throughout their stay, although there is one exception. You can still charge guests a security deposit if you manage your listing with API-connected software. It is completely up to you whether or not you want to charge a security deposit, but if you are worried that your guests may damage or break something, it is a good idea. It helps keep the guests accountable for your property because they know that they will not get their money back if they damage something.

Over and above your house rules, there are other booking policies you'll need to consider and decide on prior to publishing your listing. Thinking about these policies is really important because it helps protect you and your property. It also allows the guest to understand exactly what is expected of them so that there are no miscommunications and misunderstandings. The policies have been put in place to help the hosts keep themselves and their properties safe and in good condition. In the next chapter, we will go over effective pricing strategies for your Airbnb listing.

THE PRICE IS RIGHT— STRATEGIES FOR MAXIMIZING PROFITS AND INCOME

The average price per night for an Airbnb around the globe in 2021 was $137. In the US, the average was $208 per night.[1] This is due to multiple factors, but as you can see, the US Airbnb market brings in quite a bit more money. You need to understand how to price your property well to bring in the most amount of money. Your pricing strategy really does matter because this will either help you to maximize your profits or end up not working for you at all.

HOW TO FIGURE OUT YOUR AIRBNB PRICING STRATEGY

Airbnb hosts are always trying to figure out how much their place is worth. I'm sure you want to be able to make the most amount of money from your Airbnb rental. In order to do this, you need to understand how much people are willing to pay for your property. You do not want to underprice your property.

Even though you might get a lot of bookings, you will be losing out on money. You also don't want to overprice your property, because then people will be turned off from booking with you.

It is a good idea to have a look at your competition to see what they are charging. This way, you can get a good idea of what people are willing to pay in a similar area and for a similar property with the same types of amenities. When you are researching your competition, it is a good idea to put together at least six similar listings and take note of different types of information. You will want to record rates for the weekdays in the low season, the high season, weekends in the low season, and weekends in the high season. All of these will have different prices because of what people will be willing to pay for each. This is why it is important to not just "set it and forget it" when it comes to your pricing. A dynamic pricing strategy will allow you to attract more guests and maximize your profit.

You also want to check out the pricing on peak dates. School holidays and public holidays such as Christmas, New Year, and Easter will be priced higher because there will be more demand. Special events like local sporting events, concerts, and conferences will also attract more people to your area and this means the pricing will go up. If you live in an area that has seasonal work like harvesting, prices tend to go up as well. Basically, anything that's going to draw people to your area who will need accommodation is going to drive up the general market price of an Airbnb stay. This means that you will be able to charge a bit more for your nightly rates since the demand is going to be higher.

EFFECTIVE AIRBNB PRICING STRATEGIES

There are multiple Airbnb pricing strategies out there. You will need to pick the one that's going to work best for you and ensure that you make the most money from your pricing strategy. Maximizing your profit means that you have more money left over to enjoy, and you will also have more money to invest back into your Airbnb if you choose to do so.

Maximum Fill Rate Strategy

The first strategy is called the maximum fill rate strategy. In order to implement this strategy, you will need to follow along with your competitors' pricing. You need to attempt to offer the best experience in your city or area. The main goal is to ensure that you have the maximum occupancy rate that you can have. This means that you will need to offer even more value than your competitors in your region. You will then set your nightly rate slightly lower than average to continuously attract guests. Even though your nightly rate is going to be lower than average, your income will be pretty stable since people would rather choose your property over another property that is similar but charges more.

Maximum Rate per Night Strategy

For this strategy, you will be setting a higher rate for your nightly charges. This will allow you to increase your net profit from each individual booking. You should expect that the number of bookings will be fewer because not everybody will want to book at this higher rate. However, your income will be sufficient because you will be getting a maximum profit from the least amount of effort possible. Your occupancy rate will be lower than average but you can look at this as an advantage because you're dealing with fewer guests and will have to spend less time and money turning over the property. It is important not to go overboard with this kind of strategy, as it could lead to nobody wanting to book with you. You also have to ensure that you are in an area where people want to book. If you are in a remote area and people are not interested in booking in that area or there is not a lot of demand, this strategy is going to be very difficult to implement.

Long-Term Rental Strategy

Another strategy that you could implement is the long-term rental strategy. In order to do this, you will be setting your pricing according to long-term rentals, which means monthly rates instead of nightly rates. You will likely need to provide a rental agreement and conduct a house tour before confirming the booking. It is a lot more work beforehand because you have to do additional paperwork as well as promote your listing a bit more than just on Airbnb. However, once you have found somebody who is going to stay at your property for a longer period of time, you can be completely hands-off for the most part. You will not have to turn over your house until the rental period has elapsed. So it ends up being a lot less work for you in that sense.

You will also have a much more stable income because you will be paid per month rather than nightly. You will have to take into consideration that you will have to bring down the monthly rate so that it is manageable for people to pay. While people might be happy to pay $200 per night if they are staying for a long weekend, they are definitely not going to be happy to pay $6,000 for a 30-day stay.

Balanced Airbnb Pricing Strategy

This type of pricing strategy is an integrated strategy. You will combine all three pricing strategies that we have already mentioned in order to efficiently manage your Airbnb business. This is more of a dynamic approach, so you will not just be leaving your price stagnant. You will continuously be changing your pricing strategy according to the demand and the season you are in. For example, in seasons where the demand is not high, you can choose to employ a long-term rental strategy so that you reduce the risk of leaving your property vacant. Then, during seasons where the demand increases, you can use the maximum fill rate or maximum nightly charge strategy to ensure that you get a maximum profit.

The Flexible Strategy

A flexible strategy is one way you will determine how much you will be charging for different seasons and different dates. This is also called a "dynamic pricing strategy" because it's always changing. One option that is available on Airbnb is the smart pricing tool. This sets your rates based on the current market. Many people like to use this tool, and there is definitely some appeal because it means that it is less work for you. However, it can end up losing you money since it is an algorithm that sets the price and not you. If you understand the market that you are in, it is going to be better and more profitable for you to focus on your own pricing strategy.

The flexible strategy that I am going to mention now is one that I have implemented in my own Airbnb business and had amazing results from it. The highest-yielding exercise is going to be to fill up your weekdays. This can be tricky, especially in the low seasons. In order to do this, you are going to need to drop your prices from Sunday through Thursday, if they are not already booked. You will need to drop your prices in order to get bookings at the start of this pricing strategy. I know it can be hard to drop your pricing because you've put a lot of work into your Airbnb and want to get paid fairly for it. However, being tied to the nightly rate as the overall value of your property is a mentality that will not allow you to increase your income. Your goal should be the bigger picture and you should look at ways to make more money annually rather than just focusing on how much you'll be making each night.

Let's look at an example to show you how you can utilize this kind of strategy to earn a lot more money over a 4-week period than just focusing on a nightly rate. Let's say your rate is set at $350 per night. This would be on your weekends, so Friday and Saturday, and you booked out all 4 weekend dates, so 8 nights. Let's also say you booked 8 nights on the weekdays at a rate of $250 per night. Let's calculate your earnings:

	Nights Booked	Average Nightly Rate	Total Earnings
Weekdays (Sun to Thu)	8	$250	$2,000
Weekends (Fri to Sat)	8	$350	$2,800
Total	16		$4,800

Now that you have your earnings for the month, you can calculate how many nights you're not booked. This will help you to see that the rates that you had were not successful for those days. In this example, you would've missed out on 12 weekday nights and no weekend nights. So your missed earnings would be calculated as follows:

	Nights Not Booked	Average Nightly Rate	Total Missed Earnings
Weekdays (Sun to Thu)	12	$250	$3,000
Weekends (Fri to Sat)	0	$350	$0
Total	12		$3,000

Now that you have this information, you need to calculate how many nights you could have booked and what rate would have worked. Now, it is not realistic to believe that you can get 100 percent occupancy throughout the year. Let's estimate it instead at about 80 percent occupancy. You would then need to discount 80 percent of the nights that were not booked. We can discount these nights up by 50 percent so that you can get 80 percent of them booked out. 80 percent would be ten nights.

	Nights Not Booked at 80% Capacity	Average Nightly Rate at 50% Discount	Total Earnings
Weekdays (Sun to Thu)	10	$125	$1,250
Weekends (Fri to Sat)	0	$350	$0
Total	10		$1,250

By reducing the rates, you were able to increase the number of bookings and get 80 percent of your available dates booked. This means that instead of not getting any income on those days, you have now made an additional $1,250 in the month. Most people do not want to do this because they would lose out on the full rates on the discounted night. This is actually completely true. This is why you should not discount your rates if the dates are far out. You should only discount your rate as the dates start creeping closer and they're still not booked out. When dates are far away, you can keep your rates higher so that you can make the most amount of money from fewer dates. As you get closer to the dates and you see that your desired occupancy is not being reached, this is when you start thinking about discounting your rates. Your discounted rate will start getting booked up a lot quicker so that you can make that additional money. It is much better to have your property occupied at a discounted rate rather than not have it occupied at all.

Another benefit to discounting your Airbnb is that you are getting more guests into your property. If a guest really enjoys staying at your property, they are likely to want to come back. They might not mind paying an increased amount of money for a weekend stay. They might also recommend your property to their friends and family, and this will improve your reputation as well as the number of people that are staying with you. As you can see, running an Airbnb is about a lot more than simply setting a nightly rate. You have to be willing to change up your strategies and look into the long term as well.

ONLINE TOOLS

There are so many helpful online tools available to you that make things a lot easier. If you utilize these tools, you will find that creating pricing strategies becomes a lot easier. You'll have access to a lot more information than if you just rely on your own physical research. You might find it helpful to try out a few tools to see which one works best for you. Here's a list of some to do some additional research on:

- Wheelhouse
- Beyond Pricing
- PriceLabs
- Host Tools

Finding the right pricing strategy for your Airbnb can be really tricky. Picking the right one depends on multiple factors that are constantly changing. Making use of software tools can really help you to adjust and optimize your price to maximize your earnings. You also should think about adopting a dynamic pricing strategy rather than just setting one price and leaving it there. Doing this will allow you to increase the amount of income you make per month. In the next chapter, we will take a closer look at how you can deliver a smooth and effortless booking experience for your guests.

STREAMLINING THE BOOKING PROCESS—HOW TO FIND GREAT GUESTS

O ver 500 million guests stay in Airbnbs every year. In order to capitalize on the number of people that are willing to stay at Airbnbs you need to be able to streamline your booking process and find the right guests. There are certain tweaks that you can make in order to optimize your online booking experience for your guests. This will help you to avoid any horror stories happening to you.

WHAT IS INSTANT BOOK?

There is a feature on Airbnb called Instant Book. You can choose to select it or not, depending on what you prefer. If you choose to use it, then it will remove the approval process for you. Typically, a guest will request to book with you, and this will then be sent to you for approval. You can do some research on the guest and find out whether you want to approve this booking or not. Once you have approved it, the booking process will continue and payment can be made. This process can take a bit longer for the guest because you might want to find out more about them, their dates, and other situations. If you turn on Instant Book, the customer is completely in control. This will apply to all available nights in your calendar and they will be able to book as long as they have met the requirements that you've already ticked off.

Selecting the Instant Book option really does make your life easier because it is one less thing that you have to do. It also makes the guests' lives a lot easier because they can make bookings quickly. If they have a delayed flight or an emergency trip somewhere, they can simply book for the next day and know that their booking will be quickly confirmed. Guests who like this will use the filter on Airbnb so they can find Instant Book properties. You also increase your chance of getting the Superhost status because, in order to get this badge, you will need a 90 percent response rate. Your chances of achieving this are much higher with the Instant Book option.

On the downside, it removes the barrier between you and your guest. This means that you are giving up some control and don't really know who is walking through the front door. If you are not too concerned about this, then Instant Book could be a really great feature for you. If you are a new listing, then Instant Book can really help you. Your goal as a new Airbnb owner is to get as many people to book with you as possible. If you remove as many barriers as possible, then your chances of people booking with you increase. You will also show up on the Instant Book filter so that you have more guests interested in your property. With this being said, when you have the Instant Book option set up, you will need to be prepared for anything. Somebody could book today and arrive tomorrow, or even book to arrive at your property five hours from now. This option typically works better if you live close to your property or have property managers who are there to handle your Airbnb. You will also need to ensure that your property is always ready to receive guests because you simply do not know when they are going to walk through the door.

HOW TO SCREEN GUESTS WHEN THEY INSTANT BOOK

It is still a good idea to do some sort of screening even when your Instant Book option is on. The good news is that you can set conditions under which guests can book with you. For example, you can choose to only accept guests who have provided a government ID or who have been recommended by other hosts on the platform. This means that the guests have been pre-screened, and there is more information about them available. People who have ID verification on their accounts are a lot more reliable than those who do not. It also shows that they have used the platform a few times, so they are aware of the process and the etiquette that is involved with Airbnb.

It is also a good idea to have a look at the guests who have booked, even if the Instant Book function is on. You can still look through their social media and Airbnb profile to ensure that they are reliable. This will help you to have peace of mind and be prepared for whoever comes walking through your door.

STORY TIME

When you are an Airbnb host, you can't have full control over your guests and what they will be like. Even if you do extremely strict reviews, you might still end up with a bad one. On the other end of the spectrum, there are so many stories of people who have accepted guests that have no reviews on their profiles and they have been amazing. Sometimes it is just the luck of the draw and it is the risk that you take when you are running an Airbnb.

A few years ago, I decided to turn on my Instant Book function. This was just on a trial basis to see if my bookings increased. I noticed that for one of my listings I would receive last-minute bookings every now and then. The guests wanted to arrive within a few hours of booking. Once I saw this, I figured out that I may be missing out on many more of these bookings if people only search for listings that have Instant Book activated. This led me to turn on Instant Book, and I never looked back.

My last-minute bookings increased for this listing by a huge margin. I also decided to stop lowering my rates at the last minute in order to attract more people. This was because I knew that, come 5 p.m., someone would make a reservation to arrive very shortly after. In fact, I decided to increase my rate and just focus on the last-minute traveler demographic—I tried the strategy with another one of my properties, but I didn't see any positive results. For that property, I decided to leave the

Instant Book function off. I learned that Instant Book doesn't work for all properties. However, if you are in a location where lots of travelers are booking at the last minute, give it a trial run. For my Instant Book property, I had around 25 percent of people who didn't have any reviews. This was either because they were new to Airbnb or they were not regular users. Personally, I cannot recall a single instance where a guest who didn't have any reviews caused me any trouble. With this being said, I know of friends who are renting on Airbnb and have had very different experiences.

All the positive experiences I had with my guests prompted me to write some glowing reviews for them. Here are a few examples of the reviews I left:

> Stacy and her friends came to stay over at my property for the weekend. They left it in great shape and even did a good cleanup of the place. It was an amazing experience hosting them, and I would definitely recommend them to other hosts.

> Walter was an amazing guest. He communicated effectively throughout the process. I was incredibly happy to host him and his fiancée. Both of them treated the place with the utmost respect, and it would honestly be a pleasure to host them again.

The names of the guests have been changed here, but I think you get the point. These are just a few of the examples of great reviews that I left for Instant Book guests. This just goes to show you that it is definitely possible to have an amazing guest experience even if you do not get to approve them before they book with you.

With all of that said, it is important that you have a balanced view of what can happen with Airbnb. I'm going to share the stories, not to scare you, but to make you aware. You might even have a few laughs along the way. The truth is that becoming an Airbnb host is truly a journey and an experience like no other. You really don't know what kind of people you are going to meet, and even in the moment, if you have to deal with a horrible guest, it could always turn into a funny story that you can tell later on. This is not to make light of any of the bad experiences that people have gone through, but to simply reframe them in a way that is not completely negative. When you start off with any kind of business, you need to expect that there will be a risk of something bad happening. Have a look at these two stories and hopefully find some humor in them.

Justin was fairly new to running his own Airbnb, so he was quite open to allowing any kind of guest to book with him. There was a guest who wanted to pay cash rather than use the website system. In hindsight, this should definitely have been a red flag, but Justin just wanted to make some extra money. He did a quick Google search of the guest's name and discovered that this person was actually a high-profile escort. It was too late to cancel the booking because the guest had booked with the Instant Book function for that evening. All Justin could do was wait it out and see what the property looked like the next day. Once he arrived at his property, he was met with empty wine bottles all over the floor, condom wrappers in the bin, and

a whole host of other gross things. Let's just say that Justin was
a lot more careful about who he let into his property from that
day on. He also got the entire place deep-cleaned. Good choice,
Justin!

Cory Tschogl simply wanted to rent out her property in Palm
Springs, and two brothers decided to rent it for six weeks.
Everything seemed normal, and the booking process went quite
smoothly. However, a big surprise took place when it was time
for them to check out. These two brothers simply refused to
move out of the property. They decided to cite California's
tenant rights, which makes it a lot more difficult to evict them
after 30 days (remember we spoke about this in an earlier
chapter?). There was a lot of publicity on the story, and with
the help of a couple of lawyers, they left after two months and
didn't leave any damage. However, Airbnb did offer to pick up
the legal fees, which was pretty decent of them, I must say.

Finding great guests for your Airbnb starts with doing some
specific research on who you want to attract to your property.
I've already gone over how important it is to choose a target
audience and target market so that you can construct your
Airbnb experience around that type of guest. This is also going
to help you with the booking process. The people who would
be interested in your property would most likely be those who
fit into your target market. It'll make it a lot easier for you to
understand who is going to be booking with you and allow you
to be a bit more trusting to use the Instant Book option. You
should also ensure that you are investing some time into
screening your potential guests so that you can filter out any

problematic people. Even if you are screening your guests to the tee, you might still get a few unpleasant ones. It is best to mentally prepare for this so that you understand how to handle them if the situations do occur. If you follow a good process from the start, then you will lessen the likelihood of any of these negative experiences actually happening to you. This is why every step of the process is so important. In the next chapter, we are going to look at how you can use a channel manager to help manage bookings.

RENTAL CHANNEL MANAGERS

While Airbnb may be one of the more popular online vacation rental sites, there are at least a dozen other sites where Airbnb business owners can list their properties and gain more exposure. It actually makes a lot of sense to use multiple platforms in order to broaden your potential customer base. This will result in you getting more bookings for your property.

WHAT IS A CHANNEL MANAGER?

While advertising a property across multiple different platforms might sound like an amazing idea, it is not as simple as that. When you list properties on different sites, you have to be able to manage this property. The risk of double-booking is definitely high since the platforms are not all connected. This is where the channel managers come in. A channel manager is basically a software platform that makes it incredibly easy for a host to manage rental listings across a number of different platforms. They will be able to do this from one interface, so it makes life a lot easier for the host.

Not every host is going to benefit from using a channel manager. One thing you have to take into account is that this is a paid service. So you need to make sure that it's going to be beneficial to you before you sign up for one. The type of host that would benefit from a channel manager would be somebody who is managing their listings across various different platforms. It definitely does help to increase your exposure and minimize the risk of double-booking when you are doing this. It also allows you to communicate with your guests in an easy way, as you don't have to keep switching between multiple platforms. On the other hand, if you are a host who is perfectly happy with just using the Airbnb platform, there's no need to get a channel manager.

WHAT TO LOOK FOR IN CHANNEL MANAGER SOFTWARE

Not all channel managers are created equal. There are definitely some scams out there, so you need to make sure that when you invest in good channel manager software, that it is legit. The first thing you need to do is make sure that it is from a legitimate company. You can find this out by doing a Google search and seeing what people are saying about the software. The more people that are talking about it, the more likely you can trust the company. Have a look at the company's website and ensure that it looks reputable. You should also have a look to see if they are official Airbnb partners. You can do this by going onto the Airbnb website and checking out the software partners. If the system that you were looking into is not on the list, then there's a good chance that the technology is weak and it's probably not going to be of great benefit to you.

You can also visit a software evaluation website like Capterra to find reviews from past and current customers. This is a really good way to find out what people like and don't like about certain software. This will help you to make a more informed decision. If the channel manager software that you are looking into comes from a company that is integrated with a bigger booking website such as Airbnb, Booking.com, TripAdvisor, or Vrbo, then you know it's a good option.

Top Channel Manager Software Options

There are many different channel manager software packages out there. It is definitely worth it to do your research to find out which one is going to be best for you. To get you started, here is a list of the top channel manager software options:

- Avantio
- Hospitable
- Hostaway
- Hosthub
- iGMS
- Lodgify
- OwnerRez
- Rentals United
- SiteMinder

- Uplisting
- Zeevou

One way to help you scale up your Airbnb business or maximize occupancy for a listing is to use a channel manager. This can help you to get your listing on many other rental platforms that are similar to Airbnb. Getting more exposure is always a good thing because it means an increase in revenue. You will also get your name out there on multiple different platforms so people will recognize you and your property. In the next chapter, we will start looking at what goes into high-performing listings. This way, you can start to replicate that in your own business.

STAGE 5

GETTING NOTICED

20

HOW TO CREATE YOUR FIRST AIRBNB LISTING

Nobody counts the number of ads you run; they just remember the impression you make.

— BILL BERNBACH

HOW TO LIST ON AIRBNB

Understanding how to list your Airbnb property on the website is really important. The good news is that it is pretty easy to do so. The platform basically guides you through the whole process as you progress. This means that it is incredibly user-friendly and you are not likely to mess up or miss any important information.

The first step is going to be to create your account. Once this is done, you can start to add your listing. You will select the "add a listing" option that's on the top right corner of the homepage. From here, you will be directed to a form that you will need to fill in with the general criteria of your property including:

- **Home type**: This is basically whether your property is an entire place, a private room, or a shared room. We have already discussed this in detail, so you should know the type of property that you have.
- **Number of guests**: This is the maximum number of people that can be accommodated by your listing.
- **City**: This one is pretty self-explanatory. Once you select your city, Airbnb will give you an estimate of what you can expect to earn per month based on the information you have already provided.

Once you have filled in all of this, you can click over to the next part of the process. On this page, you need to provide some specific details about your listing and property. You will be given a selection of descriptions to choose from, and you will choose the most accurate type. Then you'll have to further specify the description from a drop-down menu. As you move along in this process, you will be guided to add more information about your listing, including things like the address, amenities, number of beds, and number of bathrooms. This is quite a lengthy list of things that you are going to need to check off, but make sure that you are choosing the right options. You will be able to edit it once you are finished, so you don't have to stress about it being final.

You will also need to include high-quality photos, a description, and an amazing title. We are going to get more in-depth into these things in the later chapters, so for now, just know that these are things that are required of you. Make sure that you are filling out your profile completely so that your guests have as much information available to them as possible. This makes you seem a lot more trustworthy and you'll definitely get a lot more bookings and interested guests for your property.

OTHER SHORT-TERM RENTAL PLATFORMS

As I mentioned before, there are plenty of other short-term rental platforms that you can use. You can definitely do some in-depth research on these different platforms to see what they offer and if you would like to list your property on them. I'm going to give you a quick overview of the best ones so that you can understand them better.

Vrbo

This stands for vacation rental by owner. It only offers apartments and private homes, so if you have other types of properties, you would not be able to use this platform. If you list your property here, then you will also be listed on Expedia since there was an acquisition that brought them all under the same umbrella company.

Vrbo works on a 5 percent booking fee plus a 3 percent credit card processing fee. The policies that deal with cancellation and payment will vary depending on the property. One thing to note is that a host is unable to delete any reviews, whether they are negative or positive.

Booking.com

Booking.com is definitely a guest-friendly and easy-to-navigate platform. There's also an instant book option, just as there is on Airbnb. Since guests enjoy using the platform, it is quite a good option for you to increase your occupancy rate. There are more flexible cancellation options, which also encourages its use. Additionally, there are no booking fees for users. One thing to note is that there is a 15 percent host fee on all completed bookings for most hosts. The fee can vary slightly depending on location, so it is best to check this out for yourself. This will be charged upon the guest's arrival, so if there is a cancellation or if the guest does not show up, then the fee will not be charged.

Expedia

This is typically not the first vacation rental platform that comes to a guest's mind. This platform seems to be overlooked by hosts, but this can actually be an advantage because you can get ahead of the competition. When you list your property on this platform, it will also appear on a few other travel sites. You will be paying a 15 percent fee on each booking. Last-minute bookings are also available on the site, and things like flights and car rentals are all in one place, which makes it very convenient for guests who are looking for the best deals.

TripAdvisor

One of the most prominent features of this platform is the ability to provide feedback from the travel community. Guests love using this platform to search for places to stay. Since it was founded in 2000, a huge number of reviews have been collected. This means that most travelers will trust it. All property listings will be translated across 26 languages and appear on all 26 TripAdvisor sites. This definitely helps expand your reach so you can attract more travelers from international locations.

The host fee per booking on this platform is 3 percent. This is on the total rent, which includes any optional fees or required fees that have been specified for the property. The guest can also book car rentals and flights through the platform, which makes it very user-friendly and a favorite amongst tourists from all over the world.

Creating a listing on Airbnb is an incredibly straightforward process. It doesn't take too much work and it's really difficult to mess it up. The platform makes sure that the process is easy to follow and the prompts allow the user to be guided through the process step-by-step. There are definitely similar processes that are involved with other short-term rental platforms. Some are better than others, so it is a good idea to do trials with these platforms so you can get a better feel for them. In the next chapter, we are going to be looking at what you should optimize in your listing to get the best chance of attracting guests on Airbnb.

HOW TO OPTIMIZE YOUR LISTING TO MAXIMIZE BOOKINGS AND INCOME

You cannot get anybody to do something if they're not paying attention to you.

— BRIAN CARTER

HOW TO RANK ON THE FIRST PAGE SEO

Airbnb SEO will determine your position among other listings with the same search results. You want to be able to get to the top of the page so more people will recognize you and book with you. Think of it like Google. When you search for something on Google, you are far more likely to click on the websites that are listed on the first and second pages. Anything after that usually calls for a new search to be typed in the search bar so you can find something that you truly are looking for. The same thing happens with the Airbnb platform. If you are ranked at the top, you will definitely get more bookings because more people will see you. The good news is that there are plenty of things that you can do to improve your SEO ranking.

Getting Back to Guests Quickly

The first thing that the platform is going to take into account is how quickly you respond to your guests. There are a few metrics that are used to measure your response to potential guests. Your response rate is the percentage of inquiries that you have responded to within a 24-hour period. Your response time indicates the average amount of time that it takes you to respond to each new message. These metrics will be based on data from the previous 30 days.

One thing you can do to help yourself out is to have a few common responses typed out. Most guests will ask very similar questions so this is a really good tip to help you feel less overwhelmed and so that you can spend less time typing. All you need to do is paste the relevant answer or guidance and send.

Avoid Cancellations

In order to be in the algorithm's good books, you need to avoid any kind of cancellations. You can do this by ensuring that your calendar is updated so you can reduce the chances of having to cancel on someone. Rejections also play into this, so you need to be sure that you are only rejecting people if absolutely necessary. The platform will compare you to other hosts, so you just need to make sure that you are not rejecting more guests than other hosts.

Enable Instant Booking

By now, you already know all the benefits and technicalities that come with Instant Book. At the end of the day, using the Instant Book option means that the Airbnb platform will push your listing to the top.

Leverage Your Top Reviews

Getting good reviews: It's so important to rank high on the Airbnb SEO. It will look at how many guests you've hosted and then how many have left ratings. You want to be able to get the best reviews possible but the good news is that a few bad reviews won't really affect your ranking if you have a lot of good ones. After your guests have stayed with you, why not email them and ask them for any feedback to improve your service. If they come back with positive reviews then you can also review them on the platform in a positive light. If they have given you negative feedback and are not happy with the stay then do not review them.

Optimize Photos

Taking good photos is really important to improving your Airbnb SEO. We are going to talk more about this subject in a later chapter, so hold on tight.

Choose a Great Title

The importance of your title cannot be underestimated. This is what's going to grab your guests' attention, so it needs to be good. There is a whole chapter dedicated to this because it is so important.

Write an Excellent Description

Your description is such an important part of your Airbnb listing. It is what allows your guests to understand what you offer and if you use the right type of words then the Airbnb SEO will push you to the top. We also have an entire chapter dedicated to this since it is such an important topic to cover.

Use Social Media

You can help get more interaction with your Airbnb profile if you post on your other social media platforms. Not only that, but Airbnb will notice this and boost your rankings immediately. Any kind of external link is very useful to help you climb in the search results.

Update Your Airbnb Profile

If your host profile is updated and complete, then you are more likely to rank well with Airbnb SEO. The host looks more trustworthy when the profile is up to date and all the information is filled out.

Showing up at the top of the Airbnb search results is a matter of fine-tuning your listing and getting every detail right. You will not regret doing this because there are so many benefits to ranking high with the Airbnb SEO. You'll be able to get more visibility and therefore get more bookings. In the next chapter, we will go into more detail about how to get attractive photos for your property.

HOW TO CAPTURE ATTRACTIVE
PHOTOS OF YOUR PROPERTY

I n one study, better quality photos lead to a 17.5 percent increase in bookings. This simple statistic shows how important taking good quality photos is. At the end of the day, most guests will not be able to take a tour of your prop-

172 | CHAPTER 22

erty before they book with you. The photos are the only things that they will be able to use as a reference for what they will be paying for.

GETTING A PROFESSIONAL VS. SHOOTING YOUR OWN PHOTOS

One thing you should consider is getting a professional to take some quality photos of your property. This is an expense that you will have to consider, but you should think of it more as an investment. When you have professional photos taken, it will make you stand out from the crowd. Your property will look so much better than the other properties that are listed. You will look a lot more professional and like you truly care about putting your best foot forward. This says a lot about you and it builds trust with your potential guests.

You have about eight seconds to grab the attention of your potential guests. This number is even lower for the younger generations. This is really not a lot of time to make an impression. This is why having exceptional photographs is so important. You need to utilize that eight seconds of attention to work for you. Having professional photos taken will allow you to showcase your home in the best possible way. There is a lot of knowledge that comes with a professional photographer, and they will know exactly how to highlight the best features of your property. Things like lighting and angles can be difficult to understand, so a professional is a good option.

You might also be able to set a higher price if you have better quality photos. Listings that have photos that have been taken by professionals can command a premium of around 26 percent higher than listings that don't have this. Even though hiring a professional photographer is an upfront cost, it would likely make up for this with the number of bookings you get and by being able to charge a bit more than your competitors because your property simply looks better.

TIPS FOR TAKING AMAZING PICTURES OF YOUR PROPERTY

If you have decided that hiring a professional photographer is not for you, then there are a few things that you can do to enhance your photos. It is really important that you take the best photos that you possibly can. It is possible to get really good quality photos by using a smartphone that has a good quality camera and by implementing the tips that we are going to be speaking about now.

Organize and Tidy Everything Before You Shoot Photos

When you take your photographs, you need to put your best foot forward. This means that you need to clean and declutter your entire property. Make sure that everything is organized exactly the way you want the guests to see your property. Do your best to make things beautiful and ensure that there isn't too much clutter in the pictures.

Prep and Inspect Rooms Beforehand

Before you plan on taking pictures, ensure that you have prepared each room and that it has been inspected. You should do this even if you are hiring a professional photographer. This will just make everything go a lot smoother. You can use the checklists that have been provided for you in the previous chapters to help you prepare your home as if a guest is arriving the next day.

Use Natural Sunlight Where Available

There is just something about natural light that makes everything look 100 times better. This is why you need to prepare to shoot your photos in natural daylight. Natural light will help to enhance your property and increase the contrast, depth, and colors of your photos. Make sure that all of your blinds and curtains are completely open to allow the natural light to flow in. You should also switch on all your lights, even in the daytime. This will prevent any shadows or dark corners from showing up.

Shoot into a Corner

This might seem like a strange tip, but it is much better to face your camera toward a corner than down a straight wall. The corners will add some dimension to your photo, and you will get a much bigger space in the picture. Your room will look a lot more inviting and open. Test it out for yourself and you'll be able to see the difference.

Look at All the Small Details

The small details truly matter when it comes to your pictures. It's so easy to get caught up with all the big items and major amenities, but the smaller things could be make or break. The little things are what complete the picture for the guests, so do consider these things. Your property should be filled with personality and make your guests feel welcome. Try not to make it look too clinical; otherwise, it's not going to be very appealing.

Use Panoramic Shots

Using panoramic shots is one of the best ways to show off your entire room in one photo. If you are unable to take a panoramic picture, then try using a wide-angle lens. This will give the guests a better idea of the size of the space.

Try Different Angles and Perspectives

Taking pictures from just one angle is going to look very one-dimensional and boring. Guests will not want to scroll through 100 pictures that are taken from the exact same perspective.

Add some variety by changing up the angles every now and then.

Use Post-editing Software

There are so many different photo editing software and apps out there. Many of them are completely free and will help you enhance your pictures. You can use these apps or software to crop and edit your photos to make them look their best. Small adjustments can really help make your pictures stand out.

If you can't afford a professional photographer or would rather take photos yourself, there are so many things that you can do to help you take amazing pictures. Just make sure that you are implementing as many tips as you possibly can. Your pictures are really important for the guests to get a true idea of what your property has to offer. In the next chapter, we are talking about how to write compelling listing titles.

LISTING TITLES THAT GET CLICKS

L ots of Airbnb hosts make the mistake of overlooking the title of the listing. The problem with this approach is that they're not focusing on what every guest is going to see when they find the listing: The title! It is one of the first impressions that your guests will get of your property, and that's why it's so important. It also helps the guest understand what your property is all about and what it provides. Remember, you only have about eight seconds to make an impression, so a catchy title is really important. If you have a good title, then you will have a better chance of a guest clicking on your listing and then converting that into a booking.

SECRET TIPS AND FORMULAS FOR WRITING TITLES THAT INCREASE BOOKINGS

There are many tips and tricks that can help you write an eye-catching title. The payoff is going to be huge when your title really draws in the guest.

Secret 1: Focus on What Makes Your Property Unique

You want a title to stand out from the crowd, so make sure that you focus on what makes your property unique. Use descriptions and adjectives that highlight the unique aspects of your properties. If you have a pool, make sure this is in your title because it's something different. Perhaps your property is in an interesting location or it has an amenity that guests are looking for. These unique features can be added to a title so guests know exactly what you are offering them.

Secret 2: Take Up All 50 Characters in the Title

Airbnb allows up to 50 characters in a title. Make sure to use up all of these characters so you can give an accurate description of the property. With this being said, there has been an update to the guidelines. Even though you are still able to use all 50 characters, only 32 characters will appear on mobile phones. This means that the first 32 characters are going to be the most important. Most guests will be searching using their phones because it is just simpler.

Secret 3: Be Specific with Your Words

Generic words simply don't get you anywhere. If you are too vague, you will just get lost in the crowd. Try and choose words that are unique and really speak to your property and describe it properly. You don't want to use words that people have never heard before, but you want to make sure that you are avoiding words like "nice," "good," and "pretty." Even though these words are technically descriptive words, they basically tell you nothing about the property. Since you only have a limited number of characters to use in your title, you should make sure that you are utilizing them well.

Secret 4: Name Your Property

A really cool thing to do is to name your property something unique. Instead of referring to it as a house or apartment, you can give it a distinctive name. The name of your property should be descriptive and provide an insight into what it is. It also speaks to your target guest so that you can grab their attention.

Secret 5: Tailor It to Your Audience

You want your target audience to be grabbed by your title. This is why you need to understand who your target guests are and then tailor your title to them. If your target audience is couples who are going for romantic getaways, then you can make your description more romantic and describe it in a way that's going to appeal to that group of people. If you are targeting large families with small children, then you can make your title more fun and family-friendly.

Secret 6: Use Abbreviations Where Possible

Since you have only a limited number of characters to use, it is wise to utilize abbreviations where possible. Just remember that the abbreviations you use should be ones that people actually understand. You don't want your guests to be completely confused about what you are trying to say.

Secret 7: Stick to Proven Title Formulas

There are a few formulas that help you create very effective titles. These ones have been proven time and time again. It will allow you to draw attention to your listing and also convey accurate information that the guest wants to know.

- Formula 1: [Specific Adjective] [Property Type] w/ [Unique Features]
- Formula 2: [Specific Adjective] [Property Type] Perfect for [Experience Type]
- Formula 3: [Adjective] [Property Type] Near [Landmark]—[Distance]
- Formula 4: Enjoy [Unique Feature] at [Specific Adjective] [Property Type] in [Location]

Your listing title might seem like such a small thing or a minor detail, but it is one of the first things that your guests will come across. This means that you want to make sure your title gets them to click and hopefully book with you. In the next chapter, we are going to talk about what makes for a perfect listing description.

WRITING LISTING DESCRIPTIONS THAT MAKE GUESTS INSTANTLY BOOK WITH YOU

I f a strong title is what catches your guests' attention, then a powerful description is what gets them to book with you. The description is not a place for you to simply summarize your listing. It is an opportunity for you to sell your guests on why they should book and stay at your property over the other options they have. You want to highlight the most significant and unique features and benefits of your property and convince them to stay with you. This should be your top priority. Writing a good description is something that can truly get you many more bookings.

WHAT MAKES A LISTING DESCRIPTION EFFECTIVE?

In order for your description to be effective, it needs to draw the attention of your guests. Instead of being too salesy and sounding like a car salesman, you need to tell a story. Something that's going to make the guests want to continue reading to find out what else your property has to offer. Your description also has to be eye-catching. Something that makes guests want to learn more about your property. This is why it shouldn't be a sales pitch but rather an effective description.

Now, it can be easy to get carried away when you are describing your property. Just make sure that you are being accurate and telling the truth. Stretching the truth in your description is not going to be of any benefit to you. Sure, you might get the booking, but when they come to your property, they will see that it does not match the description. This will result in you getting negative reviews, and you just don't want that.

Your description needs to be targeted and tailored to your target audience. This is why it is so important for you to know who your target audience is. The way you would describe something to a family looking to go on vacation is completely different from the way you would describe something to a businessperson coming into town for a meeting. Regardless of who your target audience is, your description needs to be easy to read. People do not want to read lengthy descriptions of things that aren't going anywhere. Make sure that it is specific and concise but still conveys the message you are trying to get across. Try not to use language that is too complicated for people to read through. It's really not going to benefit you if your guests can't even understand the words that you are using in your description.

THE BASIC STRUCTURE OF A TOP-PERFORMING DESCRIPTION

You can follow a basic structure in order to create a great description. Here are a few things that you should definitely include in your description:

- Interesting introduction.
- Description of all the rooms.
- Describe outdoor spaces.
- Discuss the location and nearby attractions.

Your main goal when writing your description is going to be to answer the questions before your guests even ask them. A few things that guests would like to know about are as follows:

- How close is your property to the nearest landmarks and public transportation?
- How many rooms, beds, and bathrooms are available on the property?
- Is the property kid-friendly and what is the pet policy?
- What are the unique features of your property that others do not have?
- What amenities and items do you provide?
- What is available in the surrounding areas and some things to do?

People will likely skim through the description and not read it word for word. This is why it is a good idea to segment the description into separate sections. You can use paragraphs and bullet points for this. You will start off with the introduction, then in the next paragraph, you can move into the different living spaces. You can use bullet points to describe the amenities you provide. Then in the final paragraph, you can review the general location and sign off. You can also use headings within your description so that you can break up the different sections. This does make it a lot easier to read, and your guests will be able to easily find the information they are looking for.

AN EXAMPLE OF HIGH-PERFORMING DESCRIPTIONS

Title: Newly Renovated Romantic House with Ocean Views

What You Will Love

- Complete renovation was done in 2022, so everything is brand new.
- Breezy coastal decor.
- Gourmet, fully equipped kitchen with stainless steel appliances.
- Beach access is just one block away.
- Private outdoor space with barbecue.
- Beautiful deck to enjoy the ocean views.
- Can use as a remote workstation with Wi-Fi.

About the Property

This beautiful house is steps away from the gorgeous coastline, so you can smell the salty air every time you take a breath. It is located in a peaceful area, so you will not be disturbed when you enjoy your morning coffee on the deck.

The lounge and living spaces display works by local artists and coastal decor that has been designed by local woodworkers. With three bedrooms and two full bathrooms, there is space to comfortably accommodate six people. The primary bedroom has a king bed and an en suite bath. The second bedroom also offers a king, and the third, a queen. Both of these bedrooms will share a large bathroom situated in the hallway.

The outdoor amenities are simply spectacular. With a large deck that offers a lounge and dining area, you can enjoy breakfast, lunch, and dinner with views of the ocean and the sound of the waves crashing against the shore. Feel free to sit out on the deck in the evening with a glass of your favorite wine and gaze over the ocean or stargaze to your heart's content.

Getting to Know the Area

The property is conveniently located close to many natural amenities. You are steps away from the ocean and just a short walk away from a beautiful recreational park. A stunning golf course is a simple five-minute drive away.

The town is an artist's paradise with art galleries, spas, boutiques, and restaurants. You will find craft beer, farm-to-table cuisine, and delicious cocktails around every corner. The town draws all manner of explorers, so if you are looking to meet some interesting people, then one of the many bars is the place to go.

This is simply a tiny treasure of the region that everyone will come to love and enjoy. There is truly something for everyone, and it draws you in with its quiet and charming vibe.

THE POWER OF WORD OF MOUTH —GETTING PROFITABLE REVIEWS

Without integrity, no company can have positive word of mouth.

— JAY ABRAHAM

TIPS FOR GETTING TOP-RATED REVIEWS FROM GUESTS

Getting good reviews is incredibly important when you're running your own Airbnb business. Reviews mean credibility. People are far more willing to book with hosts who have a lot of positive reviews. It shows that people have been happy with the service that they received and are willing to come back. This is one of the best ways to increase your revenue and bring in more guests. With this being said, it can be quite tricky to get these good reviews when you're first starting out. However, there are many things that you can do to get these reviews and ensure that they are good ones.

Tip #1: Underpromise and Overdeliver

The first step to getting amazing reviews is to exceed your guests' expectations. This means that you need to under-promise and overdeliver. Now, there is definitely a balance to this because you still need to convince your guests to book with you. So if you are too humble with your descriptions and your title then you will not get any bookings. The key is to deliver what you promised and then a little bit more.

Your guests' expectations are going to be set by what you have mentioned in your listing. If you provide something that is even better than that, they will be delighted. It's all about adding something special and a bit different. You don't have to change around your whole property, so the guests are completely shocked when they walk through the door. In fact, this is probably a bad idea. Instead, look at a few small things that you can do that will be a happy surprise to your guests. For example, include a welcome note in your welcome basket with a few local snacks and suggestions of where they can go to enjoy their stay. This is a small cost to you, but it leaves a huge impression.

If there are any pitfalls at your property, ensure that you let the guests know about this in advance. You can mention it in your listing but frame it in a slightly positive way. For example, if the street on which your property is located can be quite loud in the mornings, you should mention it in the listing. If you don't mention it and you get a guest who is a light sleeper, they will absolutely hate the experience and give you a negative review. If you put this in the listing, they will have already expected this and the light sleeper would probably not have booked with you in the first place. This is just better for everybody involved.

Tip #2: 6-Star Service Leads to 5-Star Results

You should do your best to go the extra mile for your guests. Start thinking about how you would like to be treated on your own property. The things you would like to have done for you are the things you should provide for your guests. Perhaps you can contact them a few days before they arrive and ask if they have any special requests. You can also follow up with them during longer stays and ask if they would like a complimentary cleaning service.

Tip #3: Pick the Right Guests to Stay with You

Making sure you pick the right guests is so important. One of the biggest reasons hosts should background check their potential guests is to see their ratings and identify whether it is a good choice to allow them onto their properties. If you see that other hosts have enjoyed the guests, then there is a good chance that these are good people.

Tip #4: Take Care of Issues Right When They Happen

It is very common for issues to arise when a guest stays at a property. Even if you have meticulously planned things down to the tee, slipups sometimes happen. In many cases, it's not even going to be your fault. If some of these incidents do happen, don't panic. All you have to do is handle them as soon as possible. Most guests are not too worried if something small happens, they just want to know that the issue will be resolved quickly.

It really does help if you have procedures and steps in place to help you address any potential issues quickly. For example, if you know that power cuts occur in your neighborhood, then have a plan to mitigate this issue. You can also notify guests of common issues that might occur and how they can go about dealing with them. As long as you provide them with the resources to deal with any potential problems, they will usually be OK with it.

With all of this being said, you must remember that the guest will always be right. If they come to you with an issue, it needs to be resolved, even if you don't think it's a big deal. Guests will be coming from all different places and backgrounds. This means their standards are going to be different from yours. Being gracious with your guests is a good way to establish a relationship with them and ensure that their needs are met. If you want to get good reviews from your guests, then you need to take care of them in the way that they want to be taken care of. You must show them that you are on their side, and whatever the problem is, make sure that you apologize sincerely and take action as quickly as possible. You will definitely see this pay off in your guest reviews.

Tip #5: Try to Be Flexible with Things Like Check-In Times

Being flexible with your check-in and check-out times is a good way to get good reviews. Guests really do appreciate it when they can arrive and leave whenever they please. Sometimes plans simply do not go according to plan, and it is not possible to check in at the regular time. Perhaps a guest has arrived earlier than expected or is going to arrive much later. Having a flexible check-in time allows the guests to set their own schedules for what is going to be best for them.

The best way to implement this is to have electric locks, so your guests won't have to arrive only when you can let them in. You can set a personal code for the guest, and they can use this to unlock the doors. This is actually an added safety measure because it can be set to lock automatically after a certain period of time and it will prevent guests from losing their keys or leaving your home unlocked when they go out. A cheaper option would be a key safe lock box if electric locks are not possible. You can place the key in the box and set a code to open it so the guests have access to the key. Since you don't have to be there when they check in, it allows you to have more flexibility as well.

Tip #6: Overcommunicate

Communication is key when you are dealing with other people. It is much better to overcommunicate than to undercommunicate. Your guests are going to be dependent on you for a good experience. This is especially so if they are new to the area or have not used the Airbnb platform before. It is a good idea to be accessible to your guests so they can contact you if they have any questions or need a helping hand. Remember, it can be scary to be in a place that you do not know or are unfamiliar with. Having somebody that you can communicate with really puts you at ease.

With this being said, it can be quite inconvenient to have somebody call you for simple things. This is why it's important to predict any common issues that might arise in your home. If you know you have a very old type of coffee machine that guests could have trouble using, stick some instructions next to it or include it in your house manual. This way, your guests will have all the information they need and they will not need to call you unnecessarily.

Tip #7: Stay on Top of Upkeep

Maintenance issues can cause an undesirable experience for the guest, and this is not going to lead to a good review. This is why it is a good idea for you to take some time to turn over the property and ensure that everything is still working well. It only takes a few minutes to do a quick scan of the property to ensure that everything is as it should be. You should also schedule inspections every now and then to ensure that all of your plumbing and electronics are working well. This way, you won't be surprised by any issues down the line because you've already taken preventative measures.

Tip #8: Keep It Seasonally Themed

Different seasons will bring out different aspects of your property and the location in which you are. If you decorate your property according to the theme, it will really bring out the best in the location. You can pull the theme from the outdoors and bring it indoors. For example, in the winter you can turn your property into a cozy feeling place. In most cases, people love to feel warm and cozy when it is cold outside. In the summertime, you can go for more fun and coastal decorations to bring a summer vibe to your property. It is no secret that every season brings its own feelings and vibes to an area. You can use this to add an extra level to your property.

Tip #9: Seek Out Feedback from Guests

Getting your guests' input is the best way for you to continuously improve your services and your property. Your guests know exactly what they expect and what you are missing. Most guests are very happy to give you some constructive feedback so you can make things better. Once guests have checked out, consider sending them an email to get some feedback from them. If the feedback you received is positive, then you can go ahead and ask them to leave a review for you. If you have received some negative feedback, then you don't necessarily have to prompt them to give you a review. Also, let them know that you are going to do your best to implement the feedback that they have given, so the next time they come to your property they will have a better time.

Getting 5-star reviews is a simple matter of being diligent and conscientious as an Airbnb host. Understanding what your guests need is so important to their overall experience and to make sure that you are becoming the best host that you can be. In the next chapter, we are going to touch on what it takes to create the ultimate guest experience.

STAGE 6

BUILDING RELATIONSHIPS WITH YOUR GUESTS

20 ESSENTIAL QUALITIES OF EVERY SUCCESSFUL AIRBNB BUSINESS OWNER

Strive not to be a success, but rather to be of value.

— ALBERT EINSTEIN

20 QUALITIES OF SUCCESSFUL AIRBNB BUSINESS OWNERS

We have already spoken about all of these qualities throughout the book. This is more to remind you of the qualities that you can work on. You'll be able to find information about most of these tips throughout the book, so feel free to go back and find the information that you're looking for. More likely, you will be reminded of what you have already learned so it is solidified in your brain. You will also realize that every step of the process makes you a better host. These 20 qualities are things you already know based on what you have learned.

1. Invest in high-quality photos of your property.
2. Have enough time to devote to being an effective and attentive property manager.
3. Create lasting first impressions, especially at the start.
4. Personalize every guest's experience.
5. Be as prompt as possible when responding to customers.
6. Buy back your time by outsourcing smaller tasks.
7. Success is in the details.
8. Be willing to go above and beyond.
9. Reach out personally before your guests arrive.
10. Offer some guidance for the local area.
11. Add a personal touch to every interaction.
12. Decorate your space tastefully and thoughtfully.
13. Don't overcomplicate the process.
14. Always be clean.
15. Keep supplies stocked.
16. Leave snacks for guests.
17. Price yourself competitively against hotels in the areas, not just competitors.
18. Always abide by your local laws.
19. Proactively collect 5-star reviews.
20. Don't think, just do it.

Arguably, anyone can become an Airbnb host. But there are only a select number of hosts that are able to deliver top-notch experiences that have guests constantly raving about them. This is the type of host that you should strive to become. In the next chapter, we will look at ways to automate the booking process to make operations for both you and your guests more efficient.

WHEN AND HOW TO USE AUTOMATION FOR YOUR AIRBNB RENTAL

Automation has been regularly shown to increase efficiency in companies across industries. For example, setting up automated processes in your Airbnb business can increase occupancy rates by as much as 80 percent.[1] That is a big payoff for reducing the amount of work that you have to do.

THE BENEFITS OF AUTOMATING YOUR AIRBNB BUSINESS

Running an Airbnb rental, or just a rental property in general, requires an investment of both time and money. If you have a busy life or you have multiple Airbnb properties, then it is a good idea to start thinking about automation as an option. As you scale your business, you will need to free up your own time because you simply can't be everywhere at once. In most businesses, automation is something that they integrate, and the rental industry shouldn't be any different.

There are plenty of benefits that come with Airbnb automation. Firstly, you will be able to work remotely and still have control over your properties. This gives you flexibility and saves you time. Routine tasks that can be automated mean that you do not have to spend time doing them. You can allocate your extra time to more important things in your business and your personal life. You'll also be able to take on more work because the smaller things have been taken care of.

Automation means that everything will run a lot more efficiently and you can increase your revenue because of this. You'll be able to speed up communication with your guests, the booking process, and cleaning procedures. Automation allows you to scale and grow your business without complicating anything. There are many different ways in which you can automate your business, and we are going to go through a few of them.

Smart Home Automation

Smart home technology is the way to go. You can invest in things like smart locks, smart televisions, and noise monitoring systems. If you have smart locks on your property, then you do not need to be there in person in order to do key exchanges or to welcome your guests to the property. All of these things can be done by themselves, and all you need to do is give your guest a unique access code. Smart TVs are just a really good way to simplify the check-in process. Anybody can figure out the smart TV, and you can schedule a welcome video to play as soon as they walk in or switch on the TV. Noise monitoring is a great way to go if you have fussy neighbors. You will be notified if noise levels exceed a reasonable level and can take action to ensure that all parties are happy.

Guest Communications

Communicating with your guests is of the utmost importance when it comes to renting out your property. You need to make sure that your guests are always kept in the loop, and there are things that they will need to be reminded about. If you have a lot of guests staying in your various properties, then it can become overwhelming to try and keep in contact with all of them. You can automate this by setting up automated messaging, automated notifications, and an email welcome series. All of this allows the guest to have the communication they need, but you are not doing anything.

Pricing Strategy

We have gone quite in-depth about pricing strategy in a previous chapter. From there, you know that it can get a bit complicated. This is where pricing strategy tools can be incredibly helpful to you. You can use dynamic pricing tools and automated pricing to help you out if you do not have the time to sit and manually work on your own pricing.

Automated Task Management

If you are not the one who is performing maintenance or cleaning services at your property, then having an automated task management service is a really good choice. This will automatically notify your cleaning service when the guests have checked out. Then they can come in and turn over the property for the next guest. Maintenance contractors can also be alerted when repairs need to be made to certain aspects of the house.

You do not have to be involved in any of this, and you know that your home is going to be well taken care of.

A Channel Management Solution

We have already gone quite in-depth with channel management services, but these are also a great way to automate many different aspects of your property management. Things like promotion, distribution, and booking of your listings can be handled across multiple platforms all from one window. This simplifies everything for you so that you are not jumping from platform to platform.

You might not yet be at a point where automation is necessary for your business. However, it's never too early to start thinking about ways you can make your operations more efficient so you can spend your time on more important things and get back some of your free time.

CONCLUSION

Getting into the Airbnb business is truly a journey like no other. You are creating a way for yourself to make extra income while doing something that is really enjoyable. You open up your home or property to other people so that they can have some amazing experiences. Not only that, but you are also creating a way to make more money and possibly start a business so you no longer have to work your regular 9-to-5 job.

By now, you should have a good grasp of what you can expect from the process. You will also be able to put together a workable strategy so that you can move forward. At the end of the day, none of the information that you have learned from this book is going to be of any use unless you start implementing it. I would suggest that you start from the beginning and slowly work your way through the book. See where you can begin implementing things to make your current Airbnb business better or start on this journey from scratch.

I would urge you to commit to taking some sort of action. This could be in the form of research or writing out a list or plan. The more you take action, the more momentum you will build for yourself. Once you have reviewed everything in the book about two times, it will be time to start going through each phase of the Airbnb framework. You can start by performing a market analysis. From here, you can just continue to take action. You will start to see things take shape the more you make moves in the right direction.

If you have found the information in this book useful and valuable in your Airbnb journey, would you consider leaving me a review? This will really help me connect with more people to help them achieve their Airbnb dreams.

Scan this QR code and leave a brief review on Amazon.

Unlock the secrets to skyrocketing your rental income and bookings with this comprehensive guide to mastering Airbnb!

Your Airbnb property isn't just bricks and mortar—it's a treasure chest of untapped potential. If you only had the right map to guide you, imagine the possibilities.

You could unlock your property's full potential, transform your Airbnb business into a consistent income generator, and finally leave behind the days of just scraping by.

This is where Frank Eberstadt steps in.

He's back with his latest book that promises to be the companion that steers you beyond Airbnb basics and puts you confidently in the driver's seat.

Inside, you will discover:

- **How to research your market effectively and outsmart your competition** – identify your unique selling proposition and elevate your Airbnb above the competition!

- **An arsenal of advanced pricing strategies tailored for different seasons and property types** – navigate the tumultuous tides of seasonal demands and make sure your rental rates are always on point
- **The magic of transitioning and diversification to ensure consistent income** – you no longer need to worry about slow seasons
- **The power of data analytics and metrics to make informed business decisions** – drive informed decisions to boost your income
- **Tips and tricks to optimize your Airbnb listing and attract more bookings** – make your listing so appealing that guests can't resist clicking "book now"!
- **Secrets to building a stellar reputation and becoming a beloved Superhost** – charm your guests and earn glowing 5-star reviews with ease!
- **Techniques to automate your Airbnb business and save valuable time** – imagine spending less time on admin and more time enjoying the fruits of your success

And much more!

Wave goodbye to frustration and uncertainty – step into a future where your Airbnb investment transforms into a consistent income-generating machine!

It is time to up your Airbnb game.

REFERENCES

Airbnb Automation: 7 Ways To Put Your Business on Autopilot. (2021, June 01). iGMS. https://www.igms.com/automate-airbnb/

Airbnb hosting: 6 ways to protect yourself and stay within the law. (2019, May 13). LearnBNB. https://learnbnb.com/airbnb-hosting-laws/

Airbnb house rules: Actionable tips and templates. (2020, September 7). Hospitable. https://hospitable.com/airbnb-house-rules/

Airbnb pricing strategy. (n.d.). Renting Your Place. http://rentingyourplace.com/airbnb-101/pricing/

Airbnb rules: 6-step checklist to stay within the law. (2019, November 27). iGMS. https://www.igms.com/airbnb-rules/

Airbnb SEO: 10 proven tips to boost your ranking. (2020, February 28). iGMS. https://www.igms.com/airbnb-seo/#

Airbnb statistics. (2022, May 4). iPropertyManagement. https://ipropertymanagement.com/research/airbnb-statistics

Airbnb supplies: A complete checklist for hosts to help you exceed your guests' expectations. (2018, October 16). iGMS. https://www.igms.com/airbnb-supplies/#

Airbnb titles: Proven formulas that attract 5x more bookings. (2020, April 27). iGMS. https://www.igms.com/airbnb-titles/

Arrojado, C. (2022, May 11). *Frank Lloyd Wright homes, farm stays, glamping sites—Airbnb's new search categories feature these cool listings.* AFAR. https://www.afar.com/magazine/airbnb-unveils-56-new-vacation-rental-categories

Average Airbnb prices by city: How much should you charge for your Airbnb? [2022] (2022, May 2). AllTheRooms. https://www.alltherooms.com/analytics/average-airbnb-prices-by-city/

Best Airbnb listing descriptions: Our top examples. (2022, March 9). GuestReady. https://www.guestready.com/blog/best-airbnb-descriptions-examples/

The best Airbnb pricing tools in 2022—maximize your profits with dynamic pricing. (2022, July 9). Floorspace. https://www.getfloorspace.com/best-airbnb-pricing-tools/

Best vacation rental channel managers 2022. (n.d.). Hostaway. https://www.host away.com/best-vacation-rental-channel-managers/

Carville, O. (2021, June 15). *Airbnb is spending millions of dollars to make night- mares go away.* Bloomberg. https://www.bloomberg.com/news/features/ 2021-06-15/airbnb-spends-millions-making-nightmares-at-live- anywhere-rentals-go-away

Clark, R. (2021, October 28). *15 Airbnb horror stories you won't believe are true.* Lodgify. https://www.lodgify.com/blog/airbnb-horror-stories/

Clarkson, A. (2021, January 12). *Airbnb cleaning checklist | 5-star turnover success.* Mamma Mode. https://mammamode.com/airbnb-cleaning-check list-5-star-turnover-success/

Comprehensive list of Airbnb host expenses. (2020, December 1). Unbound Investor. https://www.unboundinvestor.com/comprehensive-list-of- airbnb-host-expenses/

Daly, A. (2021, March 12). *25 insanely useful Airbnb tips that will make you a better host.* BuzzFeed. https://www.buzzfeed.com/anniedaly/pro-tips- from-airbnb-superhosts

Dar, S. (2022, February 23). *What kind of insurance do you need for an Airbnb property?* Baselane. https://www.baselane.com/resources/what-kind-of- insurance-do-you-need-for-an-airbnb-property/

Davis, G. B. (2022, June 27). *How to be an Airbnb host: 14 tips for fast success.* SparkRental. https://sparkrental.com/airbnb-host/

Deane, S. (2022, January 4). *2022 Airbnb statistics: Usage, demographics, and revenue growth.* Stratos Jet Charters Inc. https://www.stratosjets.com/blog/ airbnb-statistics/

Debunking Airbnb myths | Top 10 Airbnb hosting misconceptions. (n.d.). Hostaway. https://www.hostaway.com/airbnb-hosting-misconceptions/

Deciding to list your place on Airbnb—legality and regulations to consider. (2022, July 18). Padlifter. https://padlifter.com/free-tips-and-resources/deciding-to- list-your-place-on-airbnb/airbnb-legality-and-regulations-to-consider/

Dendinou, J. (2021a, August 20). *How to a create a listing on Airbnb.* Hosthub. https://www.hosthub.com/guides/how-to-create-a-listing-on-airbnb/

Dendinou, J. (2021b, August 20). *How to create a listing on booking.com.* Hosthub. https://www.hosthub.com/guides/how-to-create-a-listing-on- booking-com/

Drew, R. (2022, June 13). *21 critical Airbnb house rules examples (& templates) for hosts*. Rental Recon. https://www.rentalrecon.com/host-advice-and-ideas/ airbnb-house-rules/

Duckworth, P. (2018, October 7). *Private room vs entire place*. Bnb Duck. https://bnbduck.com/airbnb-private-room-vs-entire-place/

Filippousi, M. (n.d.). *How to write an awesome description for your Airbnb listing*. Hosthub. https://www.hosthub.com/blog/how-to-write-an-awesome-description-for-your-airbnb-listing/

5 tips to earning a 5-star review on Airbnb. (2019, December 11). LearnBNB. https://learnbnb.com/earning-a-5-star-review-on-airbnb/

Fok, R. (2020, May 21). *300 days of hosting on Airbnb*. Medium. https://reneefok.medium.com/300-days-of-hosting-on-airbnb-adb48f38b0a9

A full guide to listing your vacation rentals on Vrbo. (2020, November 30). IGMS. https://www.igms.com/vrbo-listing/

Griffiths, C. (2020, February 18). *How to conduct an Airbnb market analysis*. Lifty Life. https://www.liftylife.ca/airbnb-market-analysis/

Griffiths, K. (2019, October 10). *How to rank #1 on Airbnb—the best Airbnb SEO advice*. Lifty Life. https://www.liftylife.ca/how-to-rank-on-airbnb/

He, S., & Svetec, J. (2022, March 17). *Airbnb for Dummies: Baseline pricing for your Airbnb*. John Wiley & Sons. https://www.dummies.com/article/home-auto-hobbies/travel/baseline-pricing-for-your-airbnb-271329/

How picture-perfect Airbnb photos increased bookings by $2,521. (2021, April 29). Rankbreeze. https://rankbreeze.com/airbnb-pictures/

How to ask Airbnb guests for 5 stars. (n.d.). Hostaway. https://www.hostaway.com/how-to-ask-airbnb-guests-for-5-stars/

How to automate my Airbnb in 2021—5 easy tips. (n.d.). Hostaway. https://www.hostaway.com/how-to-automate-my-airbnb-in-2021-5-easy-tips/

How to find the best Airbnb pricing strategy. (2020, October 30). Hosty. https://www.hostyapp.com/how-to-find-the-best-airbnb-pricing-strategy/#:~:text=If%20you%20offer%20less%20value

How to identify your target Airbnb guest—pro tips. (2020, July 27). LearnBNB. https://learnbnb.com/target-rental-audience-on-airbnb/

How to screen Airbnb guest in three simple stages? (2021, March 19). Hosty. https://www.hostyapp.com/how-to-screen-airbnb-guest/

How to start an Airbnb business? (n.d.). Hostaway. https://www.hostaway.com/how-to-start-an-airbnb-business/

How to take great Airbnb photos: An essential guide for success. (2020, November

24). IGMS. https://www.igms.com/airbnb-photos/#How_to_Take_the_Best_Airbnb_Photos_9_Helpful_Hints

Hrovat, J. (2021, May 24). *Our proprietary 3 step pricing formula to earn an additional $1,250 every month.* Beyond BNB. https://www.beyondbnb.io/post/3-step-pricing-formula

The inside story behind the unlikely rise of Airbnb. (2017, April 26). Knowledge at Wharton. https://knowledge.wharton.upenn.edu/article/the-inside-story-behind-the-unlikely-rise-of-airbnb/

Is Airbnb safe, reliable, and legal? (2022, March 11). TechBoomers. https://techboomers.com/t/is-airbnb-safe

Kelsey, K. (2019, September 15). *Finding a profitable Airbnb property.* AirHost Academy. https://airhostacademy.com/finding-airbnb-property/

Kidd, S. (2022, April 19). *Ultimate Airbnb cleaning checklist + free template.* TurnoverBnB. https://turnoverbnb.com/airbnb-cleaning-checklist/

Kovachevska, M. (2022, March 18). *28 amazing Airbnb statistics you should know before booking.* CapitalCounselor. https://capitalcounselor.com/airbnb-statistics/

Krones, T. (2020, July 3). *How to automate your Airbnb rental & increase efficiency.* Host Tools. https://hosttools.com/blog/short-term-rental-automation/automating-airbnb-rental/

Krones, T. (2020, August 7). *Airbnb house rules template: 15 examples of essential house rules for every listing.* Host Tools. https://hosttools.com/blog/short-term-rental-tips/airbnb-house-rules/

Krones, T. (2020, November 13). *The best Airbnb pricing tools for small hosts in 2021.* Host Tools. https://hosttools.com/blog/short-term-rental-tools/best-airbnb-pricing-tool/

Krones, T. (2021, March 2). *Is Airbnb profitable for hosts? Everything you need to know.* Host Tools. https://hosttools.com/blog/airbnb-rentals/is-airbnb-profitable-for-hosts/

Krones, T. (2021, July 5). *Airbnb photography: 8 tips to taking the perfect Airbnb photos.* Host Tools. https://hosttools.com/blog/short-term-rental-tips/airbnb-photography-guide/?swcfpc=1

Kutcher, J. (2020, January 31). *10 tips for running a successful Airbnb.* Jenna Kutcher Blog. https://jennakutcherblog.com/10-tips-for-running-a-successful-airbnb/

Lake, R. (2021, August 31). *Does your homeowner's insurance cover Airbnb?*

Investopedia. https://www.investopedia.com/articles/insurance/120816/ does-your-homeowners-insurance-cover-airbnb.asp

Lang, L. (2018, January 25). *23 things to do to prepare your home for Airbnb guests.* The SpareFoot Blog. https://www.sparefoot.com/self-storage/blog/ 20259-23-things-to-do-to-prepare-your-home-for-airbnb-guests/

Lara, J. (2021, April 24). *How to start an Airbnb. Ask yourself these 8 questions first.* Short Term Sage. https://shorttermsage.com/how-to-start-an-airbnb-business/

Lauzon, A. (2022, March 3). *Is Airbnb profitable in 2022?* Mashvisor Real Estate Blog. https://www.mashvisor.com/blog/is-airbnb-profitable/

Leonhardt, M. (2019, July 8). *82% of people think Airbnb-ing their home is a good money-making strategy—here's what you need to know.* CNBC. https://www. cnbc.com/2019/07/03/is-running-an-airbnb-profitable-heres-what-you-need-to-know.html

Manage multiple channels at scale. (n.d.) Guesty. https://www.guesty.com/ features/channel-manager/#:~:text=A%20channel%20manager%20gives% 20yous. (n.d.). Guesty.

Must-have Airbnb tools & apps. (n.d.). Hostaway. https://www.hostaway.com/ must-have-airbnb-tools-and-apps/

Nix, D. (n.d.). *The ultimate insurance guide for Airbnb hosts.* Steadily. https:// www.steadily.com/blog/airbnb-insurance-guide

O'Connell, C. (2022, June 9). *Best Airbnb descriptions to drive more bookings.* Guesthook. https://guesthook.com/best-airbnb-descriptions/

Plus vs Luxe: Comparing different types of Airbnb rentals. (2019, November 7). GuestReady. https://www.guestready.com/blog/airbnb-rentals-overview/

Protect your investment: Airbnb safety tips for hosts. (2018, November 7). Hosty. https://www.hostyapp.com/protect-investment-airbnb-safety-tips-hosts/

Responsible hosting in the United States. (n.d.). Airbnb. https://www.airbnb.ca/ help/article/1376/responsible-hosting-in-the-united-states?locale=en& _set_bev_on_new_domain=1655368744_ZDBhODY1ZGUyODc0

Russell, T. (2019, November 12). *15 tips on how to automate your Airbnb property.* Short Rental Pro. https://www.shortrentalpro.com/15-tips-on-how-to-automate-your-airbnb-property/

Safety tips for hosts of places to stay. (n.d.). Airbnb. https://www.airbnb.ca/help/ article/231/safety-tips-for-hosts-of-places-to-stay

Screening Airbnb guests. (n.d.). Renting Your Place. http://rentingyourplace. com/airbnb-101/airbnb_property_management/screening-guests/

7 tips for staying safe and secure as an Airbnb host. (2018, March 16). Fing. https://www.fing.com/news/7-tips-to-staying-safe-and-secure-as-an-airbnb-host

A step-by-step guide on how to list on Airbnb. (2018, November 26). Guesty. https://www.guesty.com/blog/step-by-step-guide-how-to-list-on-airbnb/

Suknanan, J. (2021, March 18). *Airbnb hosts shared 19 of their best tips for getting a five-star rating.* BuzzFeed. https://www.buzzfeed.com/jasminsuknanan/airbnb-five-star-review-hosting-tips

10 things to consider before hosting on Airbnb. (2020, July 27). LearnBNB. https://learnbnb.com/10-things-to-consider-before-hosting-on-airbnb/

3 biggest Airbnb myths busted. (2018, June 3). HelpHost. https://www.helphost.com/chicagoairbnbblog/3-biggest-airbnb-myths-busted

Tips on how to write Airbnb house rules. (2020, July 2). MasterHost. https://masterhost.ca/airbnb-house-rules/

Top 12 Airbnb competitors and alternatives for hosts. (2020, July 3). iGMS. https://www.igms.com/airbnb-competitors/

289+ great Airbnb host review examples (July 2022 update). (2022, July). Eat, Sleep, Wander. https://eatsleepwander.com/host-review-example/

Types of places to stay. (n.d.). Airbnb. https://www.airbnb.ca/help/article/5/types-of-places-to-stay#section-heading-0-0

The ultimate Airbnb host checklist: Everything you need to host successfully. (2022, August 17). Floorspace. https://www.getfloorspace.com/airbnb-host-checklist/

An ultimate guide to Airbnb automation. (2021, July 18). Zeevou. https://zeevou.com/blog/an-ultimate-guide-on-how-to-automate-airbnb-management/

Wade, T. (2018, September 27). *Airbnb home insurance—what you need to know.* Ratehub. https://www.ratehub.ca/blog/airbnb-home-insurance-what-you-need-to-know/

What are Airbnb's policies? (n.d.). Guesty. https://www.guesty.com/vacation-rental-guide/airbnb-policies/

What is a channel manager and why it's important. (n.d.). Hostaway. https://www.hostaway.com/what-is-a-vacation-rental-channel-manager/

What is Airbnb and how does it work? (n.d.). Airbnb. https://www.airbnb.ca/help/article/2503/what-is-airbnb-and-how-does-it-work

What regulations apply to my city? (n.d.). Airbnb. https://www.airbnb.ca/help/article/961/what-regulations-apply-to-my-city?locale=en&_set_bev_on_new_domain=1655368744_ZDBhODY1ZGUyODc0

When (not) to use Instant Book on Airbnb. (2018, March 1). GuestReady's Airbnb Hosting Blog. https://www.guestready.com/blog/airbnb-instant-book/

Why professional photography is important for Airbnb bookings. (n.d.). Made-Comfy. https://www.blog.madecomfy.com.au/blog/professional-photog raphy-a-deciding-factor-in-booking-short-term-stays

Yes, you need insurance to be an Airbnb host. (n.d.). Six Figures Under. https://www.sixfiguresunder.com/insurance-to-be-an-airbnb-host/

Zaidi, T. (2022, March 24). *Airbnb's cancellation and refund policy (flexible, moderate, strict).* TRVLGUIDES. https://trvlguides.com/articles/airbnb-cancellation-refund-policy

Zaqout, K. (2017, November 30). *What's the best property type for short-term rentals?* Mashvisor Real Estate Blog. https://www.mashvisor.com/blog/airbnb-apartment-vs-airbnb-house/

Zaragoza, R. (2021, November 26). *Conducting accurate Airbnb rental market analysis in 7 steps.* Mashvisor Real Estate Blog. https://www.mashvisor.com/blog/airbnb-rental-market/

IMAGE REFERENCES

Bezanger, J. (2021, June 5) [Image]. Unsplash. https://unsplash.com/photos/9k_gCYLoH2g

Carstens-Peter, J. (2017, Feb 6) *If you feel the desire to write a book, what would it be about?* [Image]. Unsplash. *https://unsplash.com/photos/npxXWgQ33ZQ*

Cottonbro. (2020, July 11) *Group of friend inside a dormitory.* [Image]. Pexels. https://www.pexels.com/photo/group-of-friend-inside-a-dormitory-5158945/

Dancre, R. (2020, October 27) *People signing documents for a wedding.* [Image]. Unsplash. https://unsplash.com/photos/doplSDELX7E

Glenn, K. (2018, March 18) [Image]. Unsplash. https://unsplash.com/photos/xY4r7y-Cllo

Gudakov, Z. (2021, August 10) *Red house.* [Image]. Unsplash. https://unsplash.com/photos/faBWQt9i7dg

Hendry, A. J. (2019, February 2) [Image]. Unsplash. https://unsplash.com/photos/KNt4zd8HPb0

Karpovich, V. (2020, March 21) *Woman working at home using laptop.* [Image]. Pexels. https://www.pexels.com/photo/woman-working-at-home-using-laptop-4050291/

Kayden, R. (2021, August 5) [Image]. Unsplash. https://unsplash.com/photos/ FARBiTC4Bm0

Lach, R. (2021, December 20) *Bottles of cleaning products standing on metal shelf.* [Image]. Pexels. https://www.pexels.com/photo/bottles-of-cleaning-prod ucts-standing-on-metal-shelf-10558189/

Mallorca, T. (2019, June 14) [Image]. Unsplash. https://unsplash.com/photos/ NpTbVOkkom8

Nickson, R. (2020, January 10) *The Juniper Room, Whisper Rock Ranch, Joshua Tree, California.* [Image]. Unsplash. https://unsplash.com/photos/ emqnSQwQQDo

Perkins, P. (2017, August 13) *Airbnb.* [Image]. Unsplash. https://unsplash.com/ photos/3wylDrjxH-E

Picjumbo. (2016, October 24). *Person holding blue ballpoint pen writing in note-book.* [Image]. Pexels. https://www.pexels.com/photo/person-holding-blue-ballpoint-pen-writing-in-notebook-210661/

Pixabay. (2014, February 13) *Security logo.* [Image]. Pexels. https://www.pexels. com/photo/security-logo-60504/

Schaffner, A. (2021, June 1) *Taking some pictures with my youngest daughter.* [Image]. Unsplash. https://unsplash.com/photos/n5OqZ-sDbSI

Scholz, S. (2019, May 16) *Nuki smart lock.* [Image]. Unsplash. https://unsplash. com/photos/IJkSskfEqrM

Spacejoy. (2021, April 12) [Image]. Unsplash. https://unsplash.com/photos/ vOa-PSimwg4

Tankilevitch, P. (2020, May 1) *A person cleaning the table with cleaning cloth.* [Image]. Pexels. https://www.pexels.com/photo/a-person-cleaning-the-table-with-cleaning-cloth-4440608/

Terry Magallanes. (2019, February 7). *Four Brown Wooden Chairs.* [Image]. Pexels. https://www.pexels.com/photo/four-brown-wooden-chairs-2635038/

NOTES

1. AIRBNB BASICS

1. *Airbnb Statistics iPropertyManagement,* 2022
2. *The inside story behind the unlikely rise of Airbnb.* (2017, April 26)

3. THE TRUTH ABOUT AIRBNB HOSTING— MYTH VS. REALITY

1. *2022 Airbnb statistics: Usage, demographics, and revenue growth*
2. *Airbnb statistics.* (2022, May 4). iPropertyManagement.

4. 9 SIGNS STARTING AN AIRBNB BUSINESS IS RIGHT FOR YOU

1. *Airbnb Statistics iPropertyManagement,* 2022

6. HOW TO ANALYZE THE PLAYING FIELD

1. *2022 Airbnb statistics: Usage, demographics, and revenue growth*

7. PROS AND CONS OF RENTING OUT DIFFERENT PROPERTY TYPES

1. (2022, May 11). *Frank Lloyd Wright homes, farm stays, glamping sites— Airbnb's new search categories feature these cool listings*

10. SAFETY TIPS FOR HOSTS

1. 2021, June 15). *Airbnb is spending millions of dollars to make nightmares go away.* Bloomberg

11. THE ULTIMATE CHECKLIST FOR ITEMS TO BUY FOR YOUR PROPERTY

1. (2022, March 18). *28 amazing Airbnb statistics you should know before booking.* CapitalCounselor

14. LEGAL REGULATIONS TO CONSIDER

1. (2022, March 18). *28 amazing Airbnb statistics you should know before booking.* CapitalCounselor

17. THE PRICE IS RIGHT—STRATEGIES FOR MAXIMIZING PROFITS AND INCOME

1. *Average Airbnb prices by city: How much should you charge for your Airbnb? [2022]* (2022, May 2).

27. WHEN AND HOW TO USE AUTOMATION FOR YOUR AIRBNB RENTAL

1. *Airbnb Automation: 7 Ways To Put Your Business on Autopilot.* (2021, June 01

ABOUT THE AUTHOR

Frank Eberstadt is an accommodation manager and the author of *How to Set Up and Run a Successful Airbnb Business* & How to Unleash Your Airbnb's Full Potential.

His books address property management and business growth in Airbnb, guiding readers to seek and capitalize on opportunities in the market, nurturing successful businesses on the way.

Frank is the accommodation manager for an investment group operating hotels and motels in Australia. He has established his own successful Airbnb business, and has grown his portfolio to six properties. Frank began his first Airbnb business from the ground up and knows how hard it can be to break into property listings and attract guests. Using his extensive experience in the accommodation industry, his aim is to lay out a clear, step-by-step path that even complete newbies can follow to success.

Frank's interest in vacation property stems from his many years traveling as a solo backpacker, something he now does with his family. These two very different traveling experiences have fed into his awareness of what makes a successful vacation rental, and have been key to his success as an Airbnb business owner.

Frank still loves to travel, and enjoys surfing, but more than anything, he loves to spend quality time with his family, no matter where their adventures take them.

Made in the USA
Coppell, TX
27 July 2024

35238233R00129